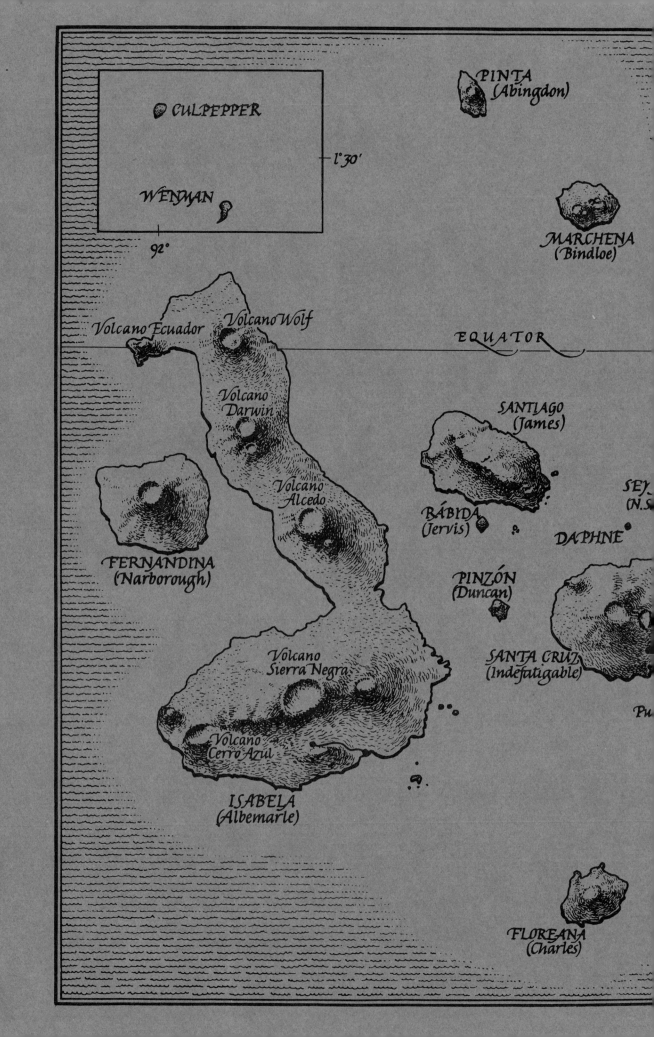

PINTA
(Abingdon)

MARCHENA
(Bindloe)

CULPEPPER

1° 30'

WENMAN

92°

EQUATOR

Volcano Ecuador   Volcano Wolf

Volcano
Darwin

SANTIAGO
(James)

Volcano
Alcedo

SEY
(N.S

BÁBIDA
(Jervis)

DAPHNE

FERNANDINA
(Narborough)

PINZÓN
(Duncan)

SANTA CRUZ
(Indefatigable)

Volcano
Sierra Negra

Pu

Volcano
Cerro Azul

ISABELA
(Albemarle)

FLOREANA
(Charles)

GALÁPAGOS ISLANDS

GENOVESA
(Tower)

N

...TBA
(...eymour)

•Plaza

...on
...ra   SANTA FÉ
(Barrington)

SAN CRISTÓBAL
(Chatham)

ESPAÑOLA
(Hood)

Miles
0   15   30
0   24   48
Kilometres

Galápagos

Galápagos

Discovery on Darwin's Islands

David W. Steadman and Steven Zousmer

Color Plates by Lee M. Steadman

●

Smithsonian Institution Press

Washington, D.C.   London

Printed in the United States of America
Second printing 1989
Library of Congress Cataloging-in-Publication Data
Steadman, David W.
    Galapagos: discovery on Darwin's islands.
Bibliography: p.
1. Natural history—Galapagos Islands.
2. Paleontology—Galapagos Islands.
3. Evolution.
I. Zousmer, Steven, 1942– . II. Title.
QH198.G3S72   1988   508.866'5   87-62629
ISBN 0-87474-882-8 (alk. paper)
ISBN 0-87474-891-7 (pbk:: alk. paper)

∞The paper used in this publication meets the minimum requirements of the American National Standard for Permanence of Paper for Printed Library Materials Z39.48-1984.

The Smithsonian Institution

Secretary   Robert McC. Adams
Assistant Secretary for Public Service   Ralph Rinzler
Director, Smithsonian Institution Press   Felix C. Lowe

Staff for *Galápagos: Discovery on Darwin's Islands*

Development Editor   Edward F. Rivinus
Senior Science Editors   Edward F. Rivinus and Theresa Slowik
Editor-in-Chief   Caroline Newman
Designer   Lisa Buck
Production Manager   Kathleen Brown

The editors wish to thank the many colleagues in the Smithsonian Institution who gave freely of their time and expertise in the development of illustrative material on the Galápagos, particularly Robert A. Defilipps, Diane Littler, and Marsha Sitnik of the National Museum of Natural History. The wise counsel of our colleagues at Smithsonian Books, especially Joe Goodwin, Editor, and Frances C. Rowsell, Picture Editor, is gratefully acknowledged.

● *Page 1: Fountains of liquid lava shoot forth from Cerro Azul, the southernmost crater on Isabela, during a 1979 eruption. Pages 2–3: Flamingos feed in a shallow lagoon beneath the steep rise of a volcanic mountain on Floreana. Pages 4–5: During the rainy season on Isabela, palo santo trees (Bursera graveolens) add a bright cover of green to normally barren lowlands. Title page: One week after a 1978 eruption on Fernandina, steam still rises over a caldera lake heated by molten lava. Page 8: The wild passion flower (Passiflora foetida) is a native, low-growing vine and a favorite of some species of Darwin's finches that feed on the plant's fruits and seeds. Page 10: A regal Great Blue Heron keeps watch along the coast of Fernandina. Page 11, bottom: A familiar sight on Galápagos shorelines: a male marine iguana displays the spiny crest and powerful claws that have inspired some writers to evoke fabled creatures of prehistory. Page 11, top: A close-up reveals the intricately textured shell of a Sally Lightfoot crab (Grapsus grapsus). Pages 12–13: "Arrested torrents of tormented lava" was Herman Melville's phrase for the harsh beauty of some Galápagos landscapes, such as this century-old lava flow at Sullivan Bay, Santiago. Page 14: The bright yellow flower of the prickly pear cactus (Opuntia echios) nestles among sharp spines and cone-shaped, fleshy fruits. Page 16: San Cristóbal Vermilion Flycatcher—See plate 42.*

Contents

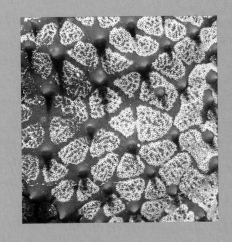

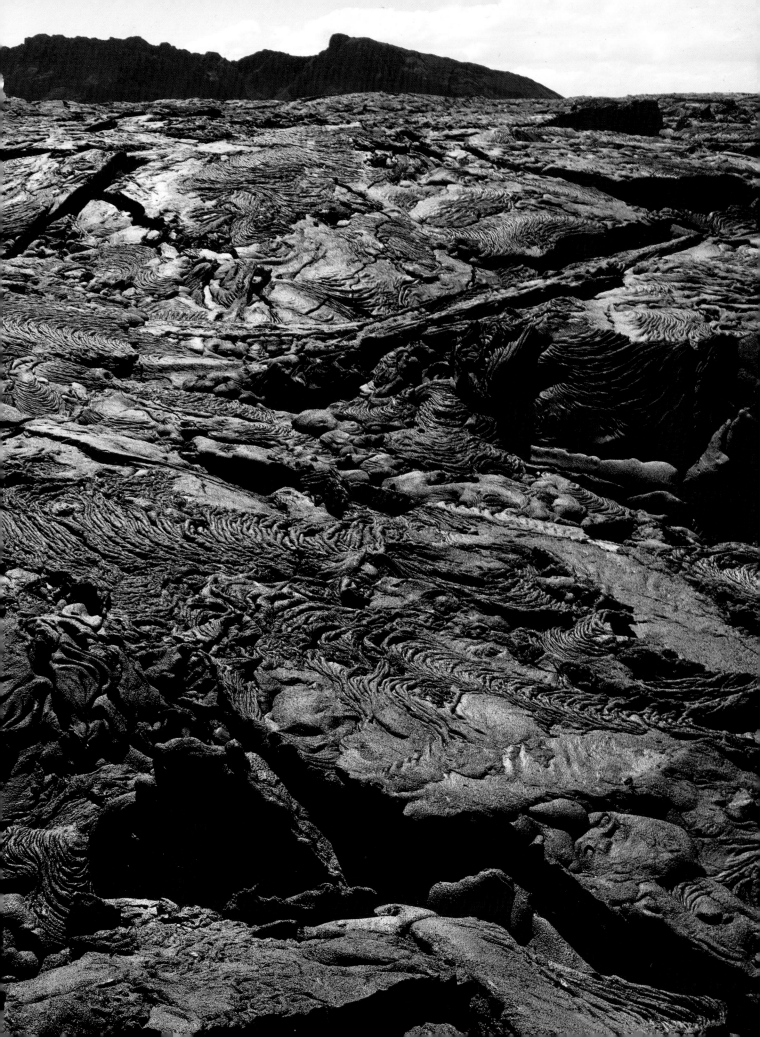

David and Lee Steadman

*dedicate this book to our parents, Norman and Theresa Steadman. Dad
was among the few persons who, at the final tally, had planted more trees
than he chopped down. Mom helped him all the way and is still guided by
a practical appreciation for nature. Wherever we are, our parents inspire us.*

Steve Zousmer

dedicates this book to Julia Ruth and Jesse Hale Zousmer.

A Word about Writing This Book

In 1986 the PBS television program *Smithsonian World* broadcast an hour-long documentary called "On the Shoulders of Giants." The title—taken from Isaac Newton's modest self-appraisal, "If I have seen further, it is by standing on the shoulders of giants"—seemed appropriate for a program focusing on my work in the Galápagos in Darwin's footsteps.

Steve Zousmer wrote the script for the documentary and later collaborated on another Galápagos film, "Galápagos: My Fragile World." He stresses that he is not a scientist and that a brief vacation in Hawaii years ago marks his closest approach to the Galápagos. Nevertheless his work on two prestigious film projects acquainted him thoroughly with the Galápagos story, including my work there, and I considered him an ideal coauthor. For this, his third book, he did the interviewing, pounded the word processor, and suppressed the arcane details and academic language that I kept offering out of well-honed professional instinct.

The focus of this book is my experience and scientific research in the Galápagos. Part 1 offers a personal account of fieldwork during eight trips to the islands. My brother Lee accompanied me on two of those trips, and his paintings illustrate the species descriptions that make up the second part of the book.

So, in a way, it was a three-man job: scientist, artist, and professional writer. Since the narrative text presents a viewpoint that is essentially mine, the first person seemed to be the right voice for the book and indeed it was our natural selection.

David Steadman

List of Color Plates

Foreword

In 1937 I embarked on a voyage with six friends from New England, two of whom had bought a schooner, the *Chiva*. The goal of our voyage, which was to last ten months, was the island of then Dutch New Guinea, where we planned extensive fieldwork. In a book published seven years later, *Trail of the Moneybird*, I took a few pages to describe my impressions of the Galápagos as an incidental experience on that long and sometimes difficult trip. It was inevitable that Darwin's legendary islands would make a strong, even if temporary, impression on myself as an aspiring young naturalist fresh out of the university. On the *Chiva*, I also had a copy of William Beebe's then-current book, *Galápagos: World's End*, and plenty of time to read in the eighteen days it took us to travel the 900 miles from Panama to the islands.

The reason for the tedious journey was that to save precious and irreplaceable diesel fuel, we were dependent on sail, and sail has betrayed many a sailor in these latitudes. Our voyage out was as characteristic for a modern sailing vessel as it had been four hundred years earlier for a Spanish bishop, Fray Tomás de Berlanga, and his companions as they traveled from Panama to Peru. At very considerable risk of deprivation of food and water, this voyage of 1535 nearly met with disaster. Fortunately, however, the bishop and his crew sailed into the path of the small Galápagos archipelago, and thus served, inadvertently, to discover these islands for the future. Our 1937 journey was similarly plagued by the dual forces of vague, undependable winds, which failed us almost continually except for a slight breeze that would sometimes spring up at night, and the counter influence of the Humboldt Current, which, arising in the Antarctic, sweeps north along the coast of South America before veering off towards the Galápagos several degrees south of the equator, off Peru.

On our placid and frustrating voyage, the first intimation that we were near the Galápagos came some 400 miles from the islands. Beautiful and delicate swallow-tailed gulls told us we were approaching the archipelago. As I described them then:

● *Kicker Rock arches boldly above the ocean's surface off the coast of San Cristóbal.*

A pair circled close to us, evidently curious about the boat. They are shaded on the head with gray masks. Their bills are large, dark pea-greenish with a crimson spot. The rest of the bird is white with a rosy tint, a forked tail, and bright pink feet. The effect is very gay and chic, as if they belonged in a ballet. Usually these birds fly in a rather effortless manner, the body swaying up and down with the wing beats . . . their voices also a characteristic "mew," low and plaintive.

After several more days of slow sailing, we at last sighted land at dawn. Off Chatham Island, now known by its Spanish name, San Cristóbal,

a great rock [rose] up out of the sea, four hundred feet sheer like the prow of a ghostly ship. At its base there is a black scar which must be a cave. The sea, flat as a billiard table, gathered itself together at intervals and, rising smooth and sleek, hurled itself at the rock. Part went into the scar out of which came a dull booming, like a far-away waterfall. The rest broke in white-of-egg streamers of foam, streaking up the sides of the rock. To one side there is a ledge on which an old bull seal lay, weaving back and forth. He plunged finally into the wrack about him, to come up quietly a few yards off. His round head stared up at us doe-eyed, the black mustachios dripping.

All these experiences came back to me while reading David Steadman's and Steven Zousmer's book, *Galápagos: Discovery on Darwin's Islands*, with its rich gallery of color plates illustrating island fauna, by David Steadman's brother Lee. Here too the authors have a voyage of discovery to relate—the difficulties as well as rewards of demanding work in the field—and they too begin with the fact of the islands' isolation, where at first glance so little seems to have transpired in these hundreds of years. Yet one of the strengths of this book is also to make clear just how much has changed and continues to change on the islands—owing not only to the slow but sure process of evolution, but also to the regrettably destructive incursions of man or the impact of unusual climatic forces.

As the first scientist to have studied the fossil record deposited in the archipelago's network of lava tubes, Steadman is uniquely qualified to track the evolutionary trail of extinct and surviving species. Ever since the days of Darwin and his pioneering research of more than a hundred years ago, the subject of the Galápagos and the evolution of its inhabitants have fascinated scientists. The sleuthwork recounted here shows once again why these tiny oceanic islands of volcanic birth should loom so large in the literature and learning shared among scientists and educators about the origins of life. The authors highlight the episodes of man's devastation that threaten the unfolding of this evolutionary story, such as the brush fires that recently burned hundreds of square miles on the island of Isabela, or the introduction of domestic animals that subsequently turn feral, causing often irreparable damage to native plants and animals so totally unaccustomed to predation. They describe at firsthand the impact of El Niño, a recurring climatic disturbance caused by an alternation in the Humboldt Current. When this happens, as it did most recently in 1982–83, equatorial currents invade the usually cool waters of the archipelago, wiping out the food chain necessary to the survival of such adapted forms as penguins and flightless cormorants. Alternations of this kind may benefit land birds and plants, but the authors show how the 1982–83 El Niño, one of the severest in recent memory, played havoc with marine forms and their sources of nutrient.

Conservation is a continuous theme in this new look at the Galápagos, and here too I experienced a welcome sense of recognition. Though I was not to see Kicker Rock again—that strange tower arching up out of the water like the prow of a sunken ship—until some forty years later, my first visit quickened my interest in enlisting international aid to arrest human threats to this unique archipelago. In 1958, Sir Julian Huxley and I wrote a resolution, passed and adopted at the International Zoological Congress meeting in London that year, calling for the establishment of a special reserve and foundation to protect the Galápagos, both in memory of Charles Darwin and for the sake of visitors and scientists to come. The history of destruction and careless vandalism in the islands symbolized to our way of thinking the perilous state of the planet and the danger clearly posed to future generations. It was our hope that international recognition and endorsement of such a foundation would lead to a concerted conservation effort, coordinated under the aegis of the Ecuadorian government. Founded in 1959, the Charles Darwin Foundation continues to thrive today, sponsoring meetings and raising money for ongoing conservation activities. With the enthusiastic support of the Ecuadorian government, two additional bodies were established in the 1960s, the Charles Darwin Research Station and the Galápagos National Park Service. These bodies, plus the recently incorporated Darwin Scientific Foundation—an endowment program established in the United States in 1985—are keeping a dream alive and making it possible for scientists and visitors from the world over to experience the fascination of the Enchanted Isles. As the following pages richly confirm, the Galápagos is indeed a unique treasure, a living laboratory of evolution unfolding before our eyes.

S. Dillon Ripley
Secretary Emeritus
Smithsonian Institution

Acknowledgments

So many friends and colleagues have helped in one way or another with my research in the Galápagos that it is impossible to acknowledge everyone. I will try briefly to mention those persons most intimately involved. The funding of fieldwork was generously provided by the Smithsonian Institution through S. Dillon Ripley, Storrs Olson, and Clayton Ray, with logistical support from Marsha Sitnik and Tom Simkin. More than anyone else, these colleagues have shown enduring interest in my Galápagos studies. Supplementary funds for fieldwork were provided by the *Smithsonian World* television program, through Elizabeth Brownstein, Martin Carr, David Clark, David McCullough, and Daria Sommers, and by the University of Arizona. Research permits and other logistical support were provided by Parque Nacional Galápagos (Fausto Cepeda, Miguel Cifuentes, and others) and the Charles Darwin Research Station (Hendrik Hoeck, Friedemann Koster, Craig MacFarland, Don Luis Ramos, Gunther Reck, and others).

For cheerful and energetic assistance in the field, I thank Camilo Calapucha, María José Campos, Gayle Davis, Uno Eliasson, Jacinto Gordillo, David Graham, Sylvia Harcourt, Harvey Helman, James Hill, III, Paul Martin, Godfrey Merlen, Mary Kay O'Rourke, Miguel Pozo, Edward Steadman, Lee Steadman, and Arnaldo Tupiza.

Museum studies were supported by the Smithsonian Institution, the National Geographic Society, and the National Science Foundation. For access to collections, I am grateful to the curatorial staffs of the British Museum (Natural History), California Academy of Sciences, Carnegie Museum of Natural History, Museum of Comparative Zoology (Harvard University), National Museum of Natural History (Smithsonian Institution), Robert Bowman Collection (San Francisco State University), University of California Museum of Vertebrate Zoology, and the University of Wisconsin Museum of Zoology. I thank James Patton, Storrs Olson, Robert Reynolds, and Frank Sulloway for reading partial or preliminary drafts of the manuscript. Other sorts of assistance and cooperation during the preparation of this book

● *David and Lee Steadman explore the interior of the lava tunnel Cueva de Kubler on Santa Cruz.*

were provided by Leslie Overstreet, Dominique Pahlavan, Susan Schubel, and especially Virginia Carter Steadman.

I thank these persons, and anyone that I have overlooked, for making the past ten years so exciting. When I first went to the Galápagos, I had no idea that the research about to begin would expose me to such a diverse group of interesting and generous friends.

D.W.S.

In illustrating this book I have received cooperation from the curatorial staffs of the Bird Section, Carnegie Museum, and the Division of Birds, National Museum of Natural History, Smithsonian Institution. I am grateful to Katherine and Al Amsler for their help in exhibiting the paintings and to Steve Simpson, Bob Dececco, and Lisa Javornick for valuable technical advice. I would also like to thank those people who—by purchasing some of my paintings—helped keep me supplied with paints and brushes. Finally, I thank my wife Lori, who never lost the faith or her sense of humor.

L.M.S.

PART ONE

I

Isolation

August 1984: Before sunrise on the Galápagos island of Pinzón, I was enjoying the solitude of early morning while writing field notes by lantern light.* I was the first awake and a cup of coffee was already brewing; my brother Lee and two local naturalists, Gayle Davis and Godfrey Merlen, were still dozing in their sleeping bags.

This interlude between sleeping and starting the day has become a pleasurable part of my routine when working in the field. Perhaps it sounds strange to talk of stealing moments of serene solitude on a remote and nearly pristine island that has never been inhabited by man, but the scientist in the field is often on a hectic schedule, with only a few weeks to collect specimens he may study for years. A few minutes of early morning tranquility offer a welcome chance to get in touch with the islands' natural pace.

Yet my ears told me we four humans were not the only intruders on the island of Pinzón; I could hear the scratching of black rats near our campsite. Looking around in the pale light, I saw several dark shapes approaching and knew there were more I could not see.

I don't mean to paint a picture of suspense and danger. While the sight of a rat on a city street may cause us to react with disgust or aversion, these rats patrolling a gentle slope on Pinzón were pests to us, not threats. Black rats devour some of the islands' most precious vegetation and wildlife, but they do not attack people. They are opportunistic predators, and they were looking over our camp as a potential source of food.

As a scientist I have devoted countless hours to finding and studying fossilized bones of rodents and other creatures. There is even one rat that I would be thrilled to encounter alive, the Galápagos giant rat, a native species that became extinct when it clashed with the very species of aggressive black rat that now surveyed our campsite. Thus when I call the black rats intruders, I have something more in mind than their interruption of my peaceful morning ritual. Indeed these rats are intruders on the island itself and its ecosystem.

Reference to individual islands follows preferred usage in the Galápagos today. A complete listing of Spanish and English island names appears as appendix 1.

About a hundred years ago the ancestors of these rats had darted ashore at night, from ships or perhaps from a single unremembered vessel that had come to the Galápagos from far away—hundreds of miles from South America, 10,000 miles from Nantucket or some other American whaling port, or 12,000 miles from Devonport, England, the port from which Darwin's *Beagle* sailed in 1831.

They were ship rats, coming from teeming harbor cities to a virgin island that had never known such predators and had no defense against their strategies. Like barbarian invaders, the black rats had an overwhelming effect on the wildlife of the island, killing Galápagos Doves, lava lizards, and other small animals. Among their most vulnerable targets were the eggs and hatchlings of the magnificent giant tortoises. While suppressing the tortoises' reproduction, they reproduced themselves in incalculable numbers. To this day there is no effective method for eradicating them.

Certainly no tactic could be less effective than the one I tried—hurling stones at vague, scurrying shapes. I felt around in the dim light for a missile of decent weight, which I winged at the closest rat. It recoiled but did not run, so I fired another rock, which skittered past it. My next strategy was direct attack: abandoning my coffee and notebook I charged the rats, which at last turned and bolted.

Knowing that further pursuit was useless, I gave up the chase. My futile irritation at the rats' presence faded quickly in the short walk back to the campsite as I watched the colors of dawn coming up over the ocean in a routinely spectacular Pacific morning.

Isolation is the key to understanding the arrival and evolution of plants and animals in the Galápagos. There is a great range of variation in how accessible the islands have been to potential colonizing species. Isolation is also the key to understanding the historical role of the Galápagos in evolutionary thinking. Though it is easy enough to fly to the Galápagos today, when Charles Darwin first visited the islands they were much less accessible and largely untrammeled. Evolutionary tracks could be found and followed, unobscured by the myriad criss-crossings of busier places, especially the havoc-wreaking traffic of human beings. Relatively speaking, this is still true of the islands today, making them an important resource for the ongoing study of evolution since Darwin's time.

The islands are also geologically young and in a relatively early state of evolution. In some cases the evolutionary process is so obvious it leaps out at you like a full-color illustration, and in many ways Darwin could not have come to a more perfect place. The irony is that Darwin did not understand the meaning of what he had seen

● *Preceding page, volcanic cinders dot a barren, almost lunar landscape on Bartolomé, a small satellite island east of Santiago.*

in the Galápagos until *after* the *Beagle* sailed away from the islands in the fall of 1835.

Think of the Galápagos as a small archipelago that stands by itself in an oceanic vastness in which there is *nothing else,* just thousands of square miles of water. The Pacific coast of South America is the closest land, 600 miles from the easternmost tip of the islands. The number of islands is variously given between thirteen and seventeen (my own count is sixteen), depending on whether islands of marginal size are counted among the full-fledged islands or among the numerous islets and protruding rocks. Their total land area is less than half that of the Hawaiian Islands.

Though the archipelago is on the equator, its climate is much cooler than its latitude would suggest, thanks to a cold ocean current running up from the Antarctic. The weather is temperate and comfortable, with an average temperature in the 70s (Fahrenheit). The year begins with a wet and rather sultry season of about four months; the rest of the year is dry and cool. A feature of the dry and cool period is the *garúa*—a fog that sometimes blankets the highlands, transforming the bleak landscape into images that evoke the misty scenes of prehistory. Meanwhile, weather that fits our normal concept of the equatorial, including tropical storms and wilting heat, occurs several hundred miles to the north.

Visitors have always assumed that the islands are basically similar, but in fact there are important differences; no two islands are alike. This became a crucial clue to Darwin, who would ultimately realize

● *A colony of brachycereus cactus* (Brachycereus nesioticus) *takes root among a network of fresh lava coils on Fernandina. In the distance, volcanic peaks rise above the gentle horizon of Isabela.*

27

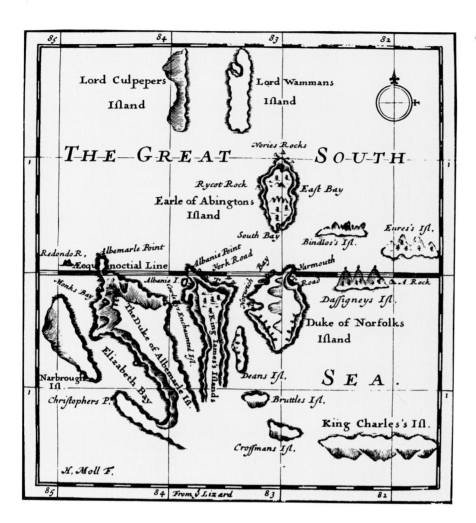

that evolution had taken different directions on different islands, as if the islands were separated by great distances rather than an average of 10 to 40 miles. Most of the islands are located in a central cluster; there are only a few outlying islands from which all other islands are out of sight.

Today the normal mode of interisland travel is by small Ecuadorian fishing boat (or by tourist boat). Before motor-driven boats, there was an element of tension and unpredictability to island crossings. Winds and currents often worked in diabolical combination to leave a sailing vessel helplessly adrift for days or weeks, unable to reach a shore that beckoned from only a short distance—a tormenting experience for crews that had exhausted their fresh water and needed desperately to replenish ashore. Indeed, the earliest sailors to visit the islands believed that it was not their ships that were drifting but the islands themselves, receding even as they were approached. For this reason, and not for any reason of beauty, the islands were known for a time as *Las Encantadas,* meaning enchanted in the sense of bewitched.

As hard as it may have been to reach the islands once they were in sight, it was even more difficult to reach them from far away. They were not only tiny dots—they were dots in a place where no vessel wanted to be. Primitive navigators prudently stayed within sight of the coastal landmarks of South America; those who ventured hundreds of miles into empty ocean lived dangerously and often briefly.

The first humans in the islands may have been Peruvian Indians, although the evidence is sketchy. Some pottery fragments have been found and identified by Thor Heyerdahl. According to Indian legend, a somewhat more official visit took place around 1485 when one of the great kings of the Incas either sent an expedition or visited the islands himself.

The first European eyes to see the Galápagos belonged to the crew of a ship carrying a Spanish bishop on a political mission from Panama to Peru in 1535. A week into the voyage, the winds died and the ship was carried far out into the Pacific. It is hard to imagine the anxiety the crew must have felt as captives on a current taking them into a vast uncharted ocean. In addition to anxiety, they suffered from dreadful heat and thirst.

The calm lasted six days. The Galápagos appeared just as the water was almost exhausted. A landing party went ashore and, though they found an astonishing array of giant tortoises, iguanas, and seals, they did not find fresh water. Another island was in sight, and they set sail for it the next day, just as the ship's water supply ran dry. The wind failed repeatedly; the crossing took three days.

● *In his account of 1535, Fray Tomás de Berlanga describes how his frustrated and thirsty crew "resorted to a leaf of some thistles like prickly pears . . . and drank of it as if it were rose water." The succulent pads and fruits of the prickly pear cactus—in many ways the signature plant of the Galápagos flora—are a food source for animals as diverse as the giant tortoise, the land iguana, and even certain species of Darwin's finches.*

Rushing ashore, they found water they described as saltier than the sea. They spent two more days searching. One crewman died, another fell fatally ill. Then, according to the bishop's account, he said a Sunday mass that was followed shortly by the discovery of a ravine in which fresh water flowed.

The ship refilled its water casks and sailed off for the mainland, wasting time on a wrong course and suffering more agonizing periods of windless drifting. The trip lasted three weeks. Again the fresh water almost ran out; to eke out the dwindling supply, the bishop ordered that it be mixed with wine and rationed. Only wine was left in the last two days as the ship hovered within sight of Ecuador, waiting for enough wind to enter a bay.

Thus goes the story of the European discovery of the Galápagos, an inadvertent and inglorious adventure that received little attention, although it did result thirty-five years later in the Galápagos' first appearance on a map. At this time the islands were given their name, after the giant creature that dominated men's impression of the islands: *galápagos* is Spanish for tortoises.

The unique and marvelous tortoises of the islands played a large role in attracting the human visitors of the next three centuries. Buccaneers and pirates used the islands as hide-outs or launching spots for ambushes at sea; whaling vessels stopped to cache supplies and take on fresh water, if they could find it. But what all these sailors particularly craved was the savory meat of the tortoise—especially appealing in contrast to the regular shipboard diet of pork cured in brine.

Giant tortoises were so plentiful in the early 1800s that men could hop across the animals' shells for considerable distances. Slow-moving, defenseless, and weighing up to 300 pounds, the big land turtles were pathetically easy to catch. In a ship's hold, given not a drop of water or a morsel of food, one could remain alive for months, perhaps a year. In a time before refrigeration this was a dietary godsend for sailors on voyages that often lasted several years.

It was no blessing for the tortoises; the crew of a single ship might load six hundred of them into the hold. Over several decades, when the combined whaling fleets of America, Britain, and other European countries numbered well over seven hundred ships, this was catastrophic for tortoises. Estimates of the number of tortoises carried away by whalers are well over two hundred thousand. Tortoises were wiped out on at least three islands and several unique subspecies became extinct. Finally the tortoise populations became so sparse that a stop in the Galápagos was no longer worth the time and effort required; ships that had once dropped anchor in the islands now bypassed them.

A positive aspect of the islands' isolation is that they were protected for so long from man. But when change came, it came quickly

● *As its name suggests, Buccaneer Cove on Santiago was a favorite haunt of seventeenth- and eighteenth-century adventurers who used the islands as a base. From here they launched raids on Spanish galleons and the coastal towns of South America.*

and affected not only the tortoises. When Darwin sailed from England at the end of 1831, no country owned the islands. As the *Beagle* was arriving in South America in the next year, Ecuador claimed sovereignty over the Galápagos. By the time Darwin came ashore in the islands three years later, Ecuador had set up the first permanent human installation in the islands, a penal colony.

Darwin arrived in the nick of time, at the last moment before human settlement had the effect it always has on the ecology of islands: drastic impact and irreversible change. Species that had existed for centuries or millennia became extinct in just a few years. Darwin collected specimens of common creatures that soon vanished and were never encountered alive again.

Throughout all this time what most discouraged settlers was doubtless the islands' lack of conventional allure. Far from resembling tropical paradises like Tahiti, the Galápagos seem almost lunar. Because of their recent volcanic origin, the land surface is made up of basaltic lavas that in some areas are rough, jagged, and punishing to traverse. The scarcity of fresh water is caused by the poor water retention of the volcanic surface. Soil is thin and tillable land is sparse.

While there are beautiful places on the islands, many who have come here have wished only to leave as soon as possible. Herman Melville stopped in the Galápagos while serving as a crewman on whaling ships, but the author of *Moby Dick*, renowned for his stirring tales of adventures at sea, had only contempt for the barren islands he described in *The Encantadas, or, Enchanted Isles:* "Take five-and-twenty

• *In the course of three centuries, a steady stream of plunderers—pirates, whalers, and fur traders—decimated the once-plentiful populations of giant tortoises on many Galápagos islands.*

31

● *A fissure appears in a frozen slab of ropy, pahoehoe lava.*

heaps of cinders dumped here and there in an outside city lot; imagine some of them magnified into mountains and the vacant lot the sea; and you will have a fit idea of the general aspect of the Encantadas."

A searing put-down perhaps, but the islands' lack of appeal was a blessing in disguise. Indeed, during this century scientists have proven that wherever people find paradise, they soon create a hell—at least for the native flora and fauna. Failure to fit the popular notion of a tropical island has saved the Galápagos from considerable damage and exploitation. Even today there are no resorts, no condominiums. By American standards, "development" is paltry. Though the degree of isolation is constantly diminishing—a landing strip built by American soldiers during World War II has become an airport, providing much easier access to the islands—by any comparative environmental standard the islands are cause for concern but not despair.

My work in the Galápagos has concentrated on evolution as revealed through paleontology, anatomy, biogeography, and extinctions. I study fossils to trace the evolution of species and am particularly intrigued by the possibility of repatriating species that have been eliminated from individual islands. This entails eliminating negative factors introduced by man and reintroducing species that have become locally extinct. Even in such a simple place as the Galápagos this is a complex undertaking, but I will describe what has already been done and what might be done in the future.

Between 1977 and 1985 I made eight trips to the Galápagos. Each trip was followed by extensive laboratory study of fossil specimens I had collected. This work took place at the Smithsonian, the British Museum, and other institutions. The modern practice of science often seems to take one back and forth between humble places and mighty institutions, between adventuring in distant islands and squinting into microscopes in the lab.

The research summarized here, part of a larger effort to study the wildlife of oceanic islands in terms of their evolutionary history, draws on studies by numerous scientific colleagues. My interest in islands took a new direction several years ago following a conversation I had with Storrs Olson, a curator in the Smithsonian Institution's Division of Birds. We were discussing the idea of writing a book on the evolution of birds in the Caribbean, where we had both traveled and worked. Yet it was clear that such a project was premature at a time when a comprehensive baseline study was required before a review of Caribbean birds would be anything but very preliminary.

While remaining involved in Caribbean research, we decided to concentrate for a while on two other tropical archipelagos that we knew and loved independently—in Olson's case the Hawaiian Islands, in mine, the Galápagos. Many people might say that I drew the short straw, at least in terms of recreational opportunities. But for someone who gets as much pleasure as I do from exploring in distant and almost uninhabited places, climbing in caves, looking for answers to questions that reach into the past and the future, and drifting off to sleep on an equatorial beach with the bright stars above, the Galápagos offers plenty of occasions for enjoyable and rewarding work.

Colonizers

Herman Melville, who was so scornful of the Galápagos, wrote that the islands' "special curse . . . which exalts them in desolation . . . is that to them change never comes." And yet they have become the emblem of a concept whose essence is change—the theory of evolution.

"Another feature of the islands is their emphatic uninhabitableness," wrote Melville. Since Darwin's time, however, the Galápagos has been widely famous for its inhabitants, including some species found nowhere else on the planet.

How did these islands arise and the creatures that inhabit them arrive? In the mind of Charles Darwin, these questions took on increasing significance as he returned to his work in England and wrote *The Voyage of the Beagle*:

Seeing every height crowned with its crater, and the boundaries of most of the lava-streams still distinct, we are led to believe that within a period, geologically recent, the unbroken ocean was here spread out.

Hence, both in space and time, we seem to be brought somewhat near to that great fact—that mystery of mysteries—the first appearance of new beings on this earth.

Thus Darwin deduced not only that the islands were young but that their geological youthfulness was a link to understanding the way species evolved into new species.

The Galápagos are volcanic islands; indeed, to scientists who study oceanic volcanoes, the only volcanic field of equally compelling interest is Hawaii. They were probably formed when great slabs or "plates" of the earth's surface passed over an area called a hotspot where molten lava was streaming up from the earth's mantle and erupting through its crust.

The result, if we could have been there to see it, was the rise of an archipelago from a shelf 1,200 to 3,000 feet below the ocean's surface (and 6,000 feet above the ocean floor). Imagine the spectacular fury of lava steaming and hissing as it rose above the surface, piercing what Darwin called the "unbroken ocean" in fiery mayhem. As it

cooled, the red-hot lava would have formed basaltic rock, brittle and barren, waiting through hundreds of centuries in silence and solitude.

Some time later the older islands witnessed the emergence of additional volcanic masses. Various dating methods tell us that these older islands, such as San Cristóbal, Española, Santa Fé, Plaza, Baltra, and northeastern Santa Cruz, emerged about three to five million years ago. To the west, younger islands such as Isabela and Fernandina, may be a million years old, or even less.

To comprehend the youth of the Galápagos it helps to put its geological origin in the context of other events. The first recognizable life appeared in the sea 3 billion years ago. The dinosaurs became extinct 65 million years ago. Most modern families of birds and mammals emerged 25 to 45 million years ago, and primitive man was evolving a million years ago.

The youth of the Galápagos figures importantly in terms of evolutionary science. In the previous chapter I said that *isolation* prevented evidence of evolution from being covered over in the criss-crossings of heavy traffic; it is equally true that the islands' relative youth keeps ancestral traits from being lost in successive generations of development. In the Galápagos many species are still *in the process of change* rather than already widely differentiated to fill diverse ecological niches. Instead of distinct entities that seem always to have filled their respective niches without direct ancestors, we see them at a stage when they are modified from their ancestors but still share many common features. From an evolutionary biologist's viewpoint, the important thing about Galápagos species is that their evolution can usually be traced.

The first plants and animals to appear in the Galápagos were not new or unique. Darwin, whose geological observations were as penetrating as his more famous biological findings, concluded that while the wildlife of the archipelago originated in Central and South America, the islands were not related to the mainland by any previous physical connection. The next question is, how did the colonizing species reach the Galápagos? How did they cross 600 miles of water to take up residence on what essentially began as big volcanic cones?

Scientists of the late nineteenth century rejected this last question and insisted the islands must once have been connected to Central or South America by a land bridge or by a chain of islands that might have served as stepping-stones for species hopping island-by-island toward the western horizon.

The herpetologist George Baur was the most adamant proponent of this idea which, he argued, explained the presence in the Galápagos of animals that are unable to fly, such as snakes, tortoises, lizards, and rodents. They came by land, he said, and after they arrived, the land they crossed subsided until it sank beneath the sea.

- *Opposite, from the rim of Cerro Azul, Isabela, steep flanks descend to a vast caldera floor. Five of the six "shield" or dome-shaped volcanoes on Isabela are still active, offering dramatic evidence of the explosive and relatively recent geological origin of the westernmost Galápagos islands.*

Preceding page, a lone Brown Pelican glides over shallow waters off the coast of Fernandina. Though the smallest of all pelican species, with a wing span of 7 feet the Brown Pelican is one of the largest birds in the Galápagos.

Although the land-bridge or stepping-stone theory still has a small following today among those who believe that large chunks of land come and go more easily than plants or animals, everything learned during the past several decades about the geology of the eastern Pacific suggests that no bridge or island chain to the Galápagos ever existed. The land-bridge theory is even less plausible in light of our recent understanding of plate tectonics (explaining geological consequences of massive movements by the plates that form the earth's crust), which tells us that the plate on which the archipelago stands is moving eastward, carrying the Galápagos closer to the mainland. Thus the islands were originally that much *farther* beyond the reach of bridges or stepping-stones.

Another once-popular theory, now dismissed, was that the existing islands in the Galápagos are remnants of much larger islands or a single very large island that was divided into smaller units as it subsided into the sea. But, as with the land-bridge theory, there is no evidence of the sinking of significant land areas. In fact, the regional picture has been one of growth and uplift rather than shrinking and sinking. As for connections between the islands, it is clear that the Galápagos islands have *always* been separate from each other (the one exception being the single expanded island once formed when the islands of North Seymour and Baltra were connected to Santa Cruz).

● *Six hundred miles of open ocean separate the South American mainland from the eastern tip of the Galápagos.*

So we return to the 600-mile question. When modern man wants to traverse a similar distance, he takes a plane or a ship. If a mammal, bird, reptile, or plant were to cross the same distance from South America to the Galápagos, it would also travel by air or sea—minus the plane or ship.

The main explanation for the colonization of the islands is the presence of the Humboldt Current. This famous ocean stream runs northward along the Pacific coast of South America until, several degrees south of the equator, it veers away from the continent (its westward-veering branch is also called the Peru Current). If you were looking at a map, you could say it takes a sweeping left turn that brings its cool water flowing directly to the Galápagos, among the islands, and beyond.

The Humboldt Current originates in the Antarctic and plays a major role in cooling the islands, along with another current, the eastward-flowing Equatorial Countercurrent. It was the Humboldt Current that carried the Incas, the Spanish bishop, and other voyagers away from the mainland, on a westward course out to the Galápagos; and it is this same current that, along with the winds, delivered the islands' original flora and fauna.

The animals came on natural rafts: clumps of land and vegetation swept out to sea, floating for weeks or months before washing up on a Galápagos shore. This natural mode of transportation still occurs: in southern Ecuador in 1964, the scientist Robert Orr noted hundreds of small rafts of plant material, 10 feet or more in diameter, floating down the Guayas River toward the Pacific Ocean.

At the same place in 1983, during a period of exceptionally heavy rains and turmoil caused by the influx of very warm air and water (a periodic weather condition called El Niño because it appears around Christmas), I observed thousands of rafts of soil and plant debris floating toward the sea. A few of these rafts were the size of football fields. Doubtless they could have supported many different South American species of plants, insects, reptiles, and small mammals—potential colonizers of any land mass the rafts might reach.

Of course over many thousands of years, almost all such rafts, carried away from the mainland by the current, floated only to oblivion. Yet a few reached the Galápagos, and, like Noah's Ark, disembarked passengers of various species—many of which found inadequate sustenance or inadequate reproductive opportunity, and died out.

Yet all that was necessary to begin a colonization was one successful breeding pair—a male and female that managed to survive and reproduce—or a clutch of insect or lizard eggs in a rotten log that washed ashore. Imagine a small flock of South American land birds seized by a gusting wind of 100,000 years ago and blown out to sea,

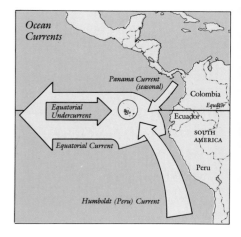

• *Though the Galápagos islands straddle the equator, they lie in the path of ocean currents that create a subtropical climate. Especially during the cool, garúa season from June to December, the Humboldt Current sweeps up the coast of South America to join the westward-flowing Equatorial Current. Originating in the Antarctic, the unusually cold waters of the Humboldt Current make it possible for such species as the Galápagos Penguin and the California sea lion to live on the equator. During the rainy season, roughly from December to May, the southern flow of the Panama Current brings warmer waters to the archipelago. A periodic weather condition called El Niño occasionally causes an influx of tropical waters warm enough to threaten the survival of some marine species.*

away from the flock's coastal habitat in northern Peru. Too weak to turn back into the wind, they face a bleak and watery future. But when they spot a scattering of small cratered islands below, they land and find themselves in an arid habitat not too different from their homeland. When the rainy season arrives, they do what birds and bees are famous for doing: they produce a new generation of their kind. A colonization has taken place.

If this happened with a different species on an average of *once in every 50,000 years*, the entire land bird fauna of the Galápagos as we know it today would have been established in only 500,000 years—half the age of the youngest islands. If such an event occurred every 10,000 years, the roster of land birds would have been assembled in only 110,000 years.

Transported by aerial or oceanic currents, life came on floating logs or random debris, by seeds or spores stuck to the feathers or feet of birds, or in the gut of some animals. Life forms unsuited to dispersal over open ocean did not survive the trip and do not appear among native Galápagos flora and fauna. This suggests another argument against the land-bridge/stepping-stone theory: a link to the continent would have meant a much more diverse selection of South American plant and animal species.

As it is, plant life in the islands is nearly as stark as the lava on which it grows, and compared with flora of the Ecuadorian mainland its variety seems impoverished. The most conspicuous difference is the lack of tall trees—there are none of the large palms, figs, kapoks, and mahoganies that typify the mainland tropics.

Similarly, the mammals that colonized the Galápagos are a small subset of those living in western South America. Absent in the Galápagos are opossums, anteaters, monkeys, carnivores, deer, and many families of bats and rodents. Successful colonizations by reptiles and mammals have occurred less than once per 100,000 years. While colonization rates are not uniform, the success rate of vertebrate colonists has probably improved as the islands have grown in size and number, developing more potential food items as the flora and fauna have become more varied.

Climate is critical to the survival and distribution of species. That the Galápagos Penguin can live on the equator is directly attributable to the cool ocean temperatures (a range of 58°–70° F in normal years, compared with 72°–80° F in Hawaii). Indeed, the only other penguin that lives as far north as the equator is the Peruvian Penguin. Marine iguanas, fur seals, sea lions, and many sea birds depend on a supply of algae, fish, squid, and other nutrients that are generally less available in warmer seas to the north. In effect, the cold Humboldt Current makes the waters around the Galápagos rich in life. In fact, cooler waters are usually more productive than warm.

● *Arid oceanic islands rarely support luxuriant forests because deep soil is scarce and the seeds of many large trees are ill-suited to long-range dispersal. Ironically, in the Galápagos the prickly pear cactus often assumes treelike forms, towering up to 30 feet in the arid lowlands of some islands.*

Below, Galápagos Penguin— See plate 11.

On land, the effect of climate on vegetation is equally important. While animals depend on vegetation, the vegetation depends on soil and climate, particularly moisture. Fertile soil is far from universal in the Galápagos: on the more recent islands where young lava still covers the surface, there is no growth. On the older islands, erosion has created topsoil, which supports vegetation.

As for moisture, airstreams and ocean currents largely determine its abundance or scarcity. The weather in the first part of the Galápagos year is affected by warmer air and sea temperatures and rain that falls in quantities ranging from plentiful to—for reasons I will describe later—catastrophic. The climate of the rest of the year is dry, but the *garúa* provides enough moisture to keep vegetation thriving at higher elevations.

Scientists recognize six vegetation zones, each generally defined by altitude. Although it should be stressed that each island is different, the system of zones is useful in describing the habitats of reptiles, birds, and mammals.

Most of the Galápagos islands support only two zones: the littoral and the arid lowlands. The littoral (or shore) zone consists of the areas near the sea or salt lagoons. Aquatic and marine birds (and some land birds) live here, along with marine iguanas and green turtles. Tiny leaf-toed geckos and somewhat larger lava lizards sometimes reside here too, feeding on the abundant insects.

The arid lowlands, occurring on all of the major islands, comprise the most diverse and widespread ecological zone and the one most visited by travelers in the Galápagos. Land iguanas and lava lizards reach their greatest abundance here, living alongside nearly every species of Galápagos land bird. Some marine birds, including boobies and storm-petrels, also nest here.

One or more of several other vegetation zones are present on the large, high islands (San Cristóbal, Floreana, Santa Cruz. Santiago, Pinta, Isabela, and Fernandina). They include a transition zone, where trees grow larger because of deeper soil and greater moisture and humidity. At a slightly higher elevation one discovers a zone called Scalesia—an entirely different world. Here it is moist and lush, with vegetation consisting of thick shrubs dominated by Scalesia trees, giant relatives of sunflowers and daisies. They attain heights of 60 feet, though 25 to 40 feet is more common. The Scalesia appears much greener than the transition zone below, which is in turn greener than the arid zone. Color differences are especially evident in the dry season when the deciduous species of these two lower zones drop their leaves.

Above the Scalesia, the next higher zone (occurring on Santa Cruz and San Cristóbal) takes its name from a beautiful bush with variegated orange, yellow, and green leaves, found nowhere else in the

● *The abundant Sally Lightfoot crab adds a splash of brilliant scarlet to many Galápagos shorelines.*

world—the Miconia. Its dense, tall stands (up to 6 feet) grow alongside ferns, sedges, and grasses in a foggy and rainy domain shared with few other plants or birds. On a few islands one encounters the extremely wet fern-sedge zone. At such high elevations (usually above 1,500 feet) vegetation can remain drenched for days or weeks, a condition that discourages most habitation.

Compounding the effects of isolation and climate is that old giant of a factor, time. The plant and animal species that colonized the Galápagos have been here for varying periods and have had varying amounts of contact with their ancestral species. A guideline in studying evolution is that the rate of change depends partly on the size of a founding population, and partly on the extent of its geographic isolation.

Thus, the smaller the founding population and the more a species is divorced from its ancestral population, the faster evolutionary changes will occur. Maximum change would be expected in a species that had colonized the islands only once and had no further contact with its ancestral population over a long period, such as a million years. Conversely, a relatively recent colonizing species that maintains regular genetic exchange with its ancestral population will tend to change less rapidly.

To put it in human terms, a man who lived in a big city and had a very prominent chin would only be a curiosity; if that man were marooned on a desert island with a woman with whom he began a family line, the trait of the large chin would probably be bred into the family facial structure for generations to come; its presence might be strengthened by inbreeding rather than diluted by the addition of other genetic material in succeeding generations.

Considering these conditions, as well as the amount of evolutionary change evident in the living species of the Galápagos, I believe the ancestors of most resident species of reptiles, mammals, and birds first arrived in the archipelago less than a million years ago. Indeed, for most species, the period of residency could be even briefer. Based on their degree of difference from ancestral populations and on the time

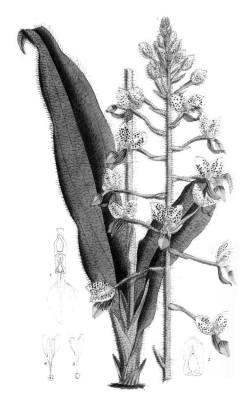

● *Though higher elevations on some islands offer suitably tropical habitat, orchids are rare in the Galápagos, partly because of the scarcity of insect pollinators. An exception is this brown-spotted native,* Punthieva maculata, *above, one of only eleven species of orchids found in the islands.*

● *Marine iguanas bask in the sun, left, at Punta Espinosa, Fernandina. The only lizard in the world that regularly feeds underwater, the marine iguana remains one of the islands' evolutionary mysteries. The lizard's resemblance to the Galápagos land iguana suggests a common ancestry, but recent biochemical studies point to the possibility of independent colonizations by distinct mainland species.*

41

of their first documentation by science, certain species of mammals and birds may have lived in the Galápagos for extraordinarily short periods by geological standards, by which I mean only thousands or hundreds of years.

Having had relatively little time during which evolutionary changes could have taken place in the islands (and *among* island populations), the wildlife of the Galápagos retains many of the original characteristics of the founding species. While most people who are enthralled by the Galápagos are fascinated by grand divergences—sunflowers that have become trees or cormorants whose once-strong wings have atrophied—scientists focus equally on the similarities among species because these help them to trace the small steps of evolution. Because these similarities are still apparent among Galápagos creatures, I believe the islands offer more promise of success than any other substantial archipelago in identifying the evolutionary relatives of resident species.

Our search for the near relatives of Galápagos species should consider not only South American species that still exist but also those that are extinct. The number of extinctions is significant—many mainland species vanished at the end of the last glacial interval, only 10,000 to 12,000 years ago. The fossil record of South American mammals includes extinct species of marsupials, ground sloths, and horses as well as extinct groups with such exotic names as litopterns, notoungulates, and gomphotheres. It is highly doubtful that any of these large mammals ever managed to reach the Galápagos.

When studied more fully, fossils of South American reptiles may shed light on the evolution of Galápagos reptiles, particularly the tortoises and iguanas. Recent studies of bird fossils found in sites on the arid Santa Elena Peninsula of Ecuador and the extremely arid coastal region of northwestern Peru—regions with more faunal similarity to the Galápagos than any other—suggest that the habitat along the coast of southern Ecuador and Peru during the last glacial interval was a sparsely treed woodland or a savanna with rivers and forests rather than a desert. This would have increased the pool of bird species that might have colonized the Galápagos.

Perhaps I have given the impression that science has zeroed in on the Galápagos and removed most of the islands' exotic mystery. This is not true, though it may be true that the mystery has been exaggerated. Largely because of Darwin's visit, many scientists have regarded the Galápagos as hallowed ground supporting species so distinct that their evolution could never be grasped. I disagree; as I have stressed, most Galápagos species retain close similarities with mainland species and are hardly too unusual to be understood. Contemporary and future scientists will devote as much attention to these similarities as

past scientists gave to the spectacular divergences that first opened their eyes to the laboratory quality of the Galápagos.

Certainly it was true that the great scientific signals of the Galápagos were on display for centuries, waiting for a Charles Darwin to arrive and take note. Yet even if the *Beagle* had sailed past the islands in its passage from South America to Tahiti, we might have reached the same insights into evolution at roughly the same time. Another English naturalist, Alfred Russel Wallace, was mulling over similar ideas and almost stole Darwin's thunder. If this had happened, very likely the Galápagos would have played a less critical role in evolutionary research, perhaps even today.

Indeed it was not until seventy years after Darwin's visit that scientists undertook an extensive biotic survey in the islands. This was the 1905–1906 California Academy of Sciences expedition, led by Rollo Beck, whose findings provide essential baseline information on Galápagos flora and fauna. Specimens gathered by Beck's group are still being studied and interpreted today.

In 1719 the English writer Daniel Defoe published the famous novel *Robinson Crusoe*, based on the story of a real castaway named Alexander Selkirk, who survived more than four years marooned in the Juan Fernández Islands, south of the Galápagos in a comparable location off the Pacific coast of Chile.

It is often said that all the creatures that colonized the Galápagos are Robinson Crusoes, although they did something Crusoe couldn't do: they reproduced. Having done so, they embarked on a humble future which would stimulate a world-shaking change of thought as mankind struggled to understand the appearance of new beings on earth—what Darwin called "the mystery of mysteries."

● *Even the ancestors of the Galápagos tortoise had to cross 600 miles of ocean to arrive in the islands. Perhaps the first colonizers were much smaller than the giants that roam the islands today, or it may be that only tiny young first washed out to the islands on a raft of floating debris. As tortoises are fairly buoyant, perhaps the original colonizers simply floated out to sea, where ocean currents carried them to the islands that would later be named for these legendary inhabitants.*

"At Last Gleams of Light Have Come..."

According to the theory of evolution all the life we see around us—every tree, bug, animal, and person—participates in a never-ending process of change through time.

The period of time is fantastically large and reaches deep into the ancestry of species. The changes are usually small and result from incremental adaptations to local environments. For instance, the Swallow-tailed Gull arrived from the mainland as a day-feeding marine bird. In its new habitat the colonizing population of gulls found a new prey—the luminescent squid that can be seen in the Galápagos waters at night. A certain amount of genetic variation was already present in the birds that arrived in the archipelago. Those with better night vision (those with larger eyes that have more light-gathering ability) were more successful hunters of this new prey; thus they had better survival and reproduction rates than the gulls with smaller eyes. Over thousands of generations some traits were "selected" as permanent features, and the species was transformed into a gull with bulging eyes superficially like those of an owl. The ancestral colonizing species has given way to a new species specifically adapted to a new environment.

The idea of evolution is itself part of an evolution in thought, an advance from the period in which the biblical doctrine of Creation laid down the law that all life was designed by the Creator, down to the finest detail. Creationism said that God's designs were immutable; changes and new life forms were added through successive divine creations, *not* by species evolving in a process of nature.

This doctrine dominated Western thought for hundreds of years. It was part of the general fabric of belief but it had a particular hold on scientific theorizing. This period in the history of science has sometimes been portrayed as one of religion *versus* science, but actually it was one of science *in* religion. As many scientists were religious men, they often attempted to reconcile their observations and theories with the story of Genesis. Such attempts ruled out the idea of a very old earth: it had been computed by church scholars that the world was

created at 9 A.M. the morning of Sunday, 23 October, 4004 B.C., so the world was less than 6,000 years old. Within such a framework there was no need to consider slow accumulations of change—all species had been created in six days and there had been no significant developments thereafter. In the eighteenth and early nineteenth centuries new discoveries and theories, especially in geology and systematics, created a tension that would increasingly call long-held scientific (and religious) convictions into question.

Publication of *On the Origin of Species* dealt a death blow to Creationism, at least among serious scientists. Darwin's findings, backed by impressive evidence, forever changed the way people looked at their world. He was not the first to think about evolution: speculation had been going on for centuries. Indeed, Darwin's own grandfather, Erasmus Darwin, was among the prominent theorizers (though the grandson later said he had not paid much attention to his grandfather's theories). But if others helped set the stage, it was Charles Darwin who refined and formulated the idea and amassed a body of evidence that could not be refuted. Others speculated about evolution; Darwin proved the theory.

One of the many consequences of what Darwin did and said was to provide me and many other scientists with productive employment. Darwin quite literally gave scientists a great deal to *do*, liberating them from a static biological doctrine and opening up an entirely new realm of inquiry, thus stimulating serious questions that will keep researchers busy for centuries to come. This is not the least of many reasons why scientists hold him in such esteem.

Darwin was also an exemplary model for the practice of science. He worked and studied so hard, occasionally bungled but recovered from his bungles, kept an open mind, did not shrink from challenging entrenched doctrine, compiled exhaustive evidence and documentation, and ultimately presented his findings knowing they would not be the last word on evolution.

It has been said that one of the great restraints on Darwin was his reluctance to crack the foundation of religious beliefs that were dear to his wife and many people he knew and loved. Darwin himself, who graduated from Cambridge intending to become a minister, started out as a firm believer. He was accepted as ship's naturalist aboard the *Beagle* by Captain Robert FitzRoy, who probably expected that the young naturalist would bring back evidence to support sacred doctrine. Both FitzRoy and Darwin were creationists when the *Beagle* left England and both were still creationists when it returned. But Darwin was no longer undoubting.

To place Darwin on a pedestal is an unfortunate way to honor him because it distorts the reality that is more inspiring than the myth. Our image of him, based on photographs taken in his old age

• *Preceding page, Blue-footed Boobies roost on the cliffs of an eroded tuff cone on Santiago, one of four islands where Darwin went ashore in 1835.*

This famous photograph of Darwin was taken on the veranda of Down House one year before his death in 1882.

(he died in 1882 at age 73), is of an elderly titan, winter in his face; bushy eyebrows and a great white beard make him seem almost ancient.

In fact the Darwin of the *Beagle* was a youthful explorer, a fresh and energetic 22-year-old amateur naturalist and drop-out as a medical student. His father, a well-to-do physician who hoped his son would choose the same vocation, was disappointed when the young Darwin proved unable to tolerate the sight of surgery. This was surgery in a time before anesthesia, and the gentle young man, witnessing operations on children, was horrified by the spectacle of agony and blood.

As a boy Darwin was an ardent hiker and collector, with a particular fascination for beetles, and he continued to collect avidly during his university years. Yet it appears that Darwin himself did not think of natural history as a calling or future profession but rather as a life-long source of intellectual enjoyment.

The *Beagle's* primary mission was mapping and coastal surveying, but it had a berth for a scientist. Darwin was not the first choice. At least two other candidates rejected the post. They had families and could not accept the separation that a long voyage entailed (the *Beagle* was away for five years), nor could they accept an unpaid position. It seems amazing that Darwin did not receive a regular salary for his service on the *Beagle* and indeed had to absorb considerable expenses out of his own—or rather his father's—pocket. Money problems never hindered Darwin; the world is forever indebted to Dr. Darwin's prosperity. As for availability, Darwin was unmarried and willing to go off on a long voyage, possibly because he had been inspired by his reading of books by the celebrated naturalist and world traveler Alexander von Humboldt (for whom the Humboldt Current is named). Darwin was also willing to tolerate the many hardships of life on board a small sailing vessel. One of the two naturalists offered the position before him is said to have been dissuaded by the size of his cabin, which had to be shared with Captain FitzRoy.

FitzRoy, who was highly intelligent, opinionated, domineering, and possibly manic depressive, at first doubted that Darwin was the right person for the job. A brilliant navigator and surveyor, FitzRoy nevertheless put great stock in physiognomy and had a negative reaction to the shape of Darwin's nose.

The Captain was fortunately won over by a quality that belonged to Darwin throughout his life: he was effortlessly likable. He got along well with people of all sorts and he brought out their generosity: whether they were eminent scientists or rough sailors, they willingly shared their knowledge with him. A shipmate on the *Beagle* later wrote, "I think he was the only man I ever knew against whom I never heard a word said; and as people when shut up on a ship for five years are apt to get cross with each other, that is saying a good deal."

● *One of the handsomest birds in the islands, the Swallow-tailed Gull roosts during much of the day and feeds only at night. The bird's bulging black eyes, set off by a characteristic ring of bright red skin, are well adapted for nocturnal feeding.*

Darwin was a lanky 6 feet tall at a time when ships were built for smaller men. He slept in a hammock from which his legs protruded into a drawer. He shared a cramped cabin and his working space was limited to a few square feet at the end of the chart table. Although he was a hardy explorer on land and regarded as a great field naturalist, he was chronically seasick. Not many people prone to seasickness would endure a five-year voyage, let alone be considered an affable shipmate.

The *Beagle* crossed the South Atlantic and sailed down the Atlantic coast of South America, rounding Cape Horn and coming up the Pacific coast. Considerable time was spent in excursions ashore where Darwin studied plants and animals and developed a zealous interest in geology and paleontology. He returned from these excursions laden with specimens—Captain FitzRoy later wrote of being amused by the "cargoes of apparent rubbish" brought back to the ship by Darwin

● *The* Beagle *lies at anchor in Beagle Channel, Tierra del Fuego, before beginning its journey up the west coast of South America.*

and his servant, Syms Covington; but FitzRoy was also impressed by the earnestness of Darwin's studies. Soon the many crates of specimens shipped back to Britain won Darwin the respect of his scientific peers and established him as a capable naturalist with a bright future.

The voyage was in its fourth year when the *Beagle* turned westward, stopping in the Galápagos on its way to the South Seas. Darwin went ashore on the island of Chatham (most of the islands are now called by their Spanish names—Chatham is San Cristóbal) on 17 September 1835.

"Nothing could be less inviting than the first appearance," he wrote, describing the rough, parched surface of a black lava field which, heated by the noonday sun, "gave to the air a close and sultry feeling, like that from a stove. . . . The entire surface . . . seems to have been permeated like a sieve by the subterranean vapors: here and there the lava, whilst soft, had been blown into great bubbles; and in other parts the tops of caverns similarly formed have fallen in, leaving circular pits with steep sides." He tried to collect plants but got only "wretched-looking little weeds."

On another day he went ashore and had his first encounter with the extraordinary wildlife of the Galápagos:

The day was glowing hot, and the scrambling over the rough surfaces and through the intricate thickets was very fatiguing; but I was well repaid by the strange Cyclopean scene. As I was walking along I met two large tortoises, each of which must have weighed at least two hundred pounds: one was eating a piece of cactus and as I approached, it stared at me and slowly stalked away; the other gave a deep hiss, and drew in its head. These huge reptiles, surrounded by the black lava, the leafless shrubs, and large cacti, seemed to my fancy like some antediluvian animals.

The quotation suggests some of the impact the islands must have had on the 26-year-old Darwin. All to himself he had a group of islands where no other scientist had ever set foot. Fabulous creatures that were unknown to science, like the giant tortoises and land iguanas, presented themselves for his inspection.

Part of this impact, as indicated by the variety of specimens the *Beagle* shipped home, had to do with the sheer range of Darwin's scientific interests. During the voyage Darwin had occasion to collect and observe in many areas—geology, paleontology, zoology, and botany. The growing breadth of his outlook, the freedom to relate ideas from a number of disciplines, was the key to his seeing what specialists overlooked. Others saw trees and some glimpsed the forest, but Darwin saw the forest *and* the trees and studied both with equal zeal.

Darwin would have been the first to contest the myth that has come to surround his "discovery" of evolution, namely, that after strolling around the islands looking at the birds, he experienced a "Eureka" moment—a sudden insight or revelation about the origins of species. The idea of geniuses solving cosmic puzzles in flashes of inspiration—Darwin supposedly encountering evolving finches in the Galápagos or Isaac Newton conceiving the law of gravity by watching a falling apple—makes for catchy stories but they are often untrue. (Sometimes insight *is* an important factor; I will later mention another scientist who perceived the key to evolution in the course of a high-fevered fit of malaria, conceptually catching up with what cost Darwin two decades of careful study.)

In several penetrating studies, the eminent Darwin scholar Frank Sulloway has recently shown that Darwin did not even come close to a Eureka moment in the islands. He was not looking for proof of evolution and he did not realize he had found it until long after the *Beagle* had left the archipelago. Indeed, Darwin came face to face in

the Galápagos with several good clues that he failed to appreciate. He made numerous blunders in collecting and labeling specimens. Back in England in later years he must have cursed himself for obvious errors, such as taking part in eating the thirty tortoises the *Beagle* took on as food and then not thinking twice as the scientifically important but inedible carapaces were tossed overboard. Darwin mistakenly thought the tortoises he saw in the Galápagos were not native to the archipelago. Having visited the islands that were named and celebrated for their most striking inhabitants, the *Beagle* went home without a single adult tortoise specimen.

One limit on Darwin's work as a scientist is obvious but often overlooked: *he couldn't go back.* There were no airliners to jet him down to the islands so he could patch up a few mistakes; the five years on the *Beagle* constituted the travel of a lifetime. It cost Darwin a huge effort to try to straighten out the labeling mess, to fill in blanks that could have been filled in fairly easily in the islands, to work without specimens that would have made his studies so much more direct and certain. Every scientist makes mistakes while out in the field—typically involving things left undone or ideas overlooked—

● *Darwin and the crew of the* Beagle *first stepped on Galápagos shores at Stephen's Bay, San Cristóbal, in September 1835.*

● *Opposite, a wealth of specimens collected during the* Beagle's *five-year voyage bears witness to Darwin's keen interest in paleontology. In Argentina he was amazed to discover fossil remains of gigantic quadrupeds previously unknown to science, including this nearly complete skull of the extinct* Toxodon platensis.

• *These early views of four Galápagos islands visited by the Beagle were published in Captain FitzRoy's account of the voyage. Today the islands are known by their Spanish names, from top to bottom, Floreana, San Cristóbal, Santiago, and Isabela.*

but there is usually the possibility of a second trip, this time with the benefit of hindsight.

Darwin's errors are understandable enough given that he was not looking for proof of evolution in 1835. He had no thoughts of unravelling the "mystery of mysteries," no consciousness of becoming the star actor in a momentous drama. He was only a young scientist looking for interesting things and often finding them. He spent nineteen days of exploration ashore in the islands and eighteen days cruising between them on the *Beagle*. He visited only four of the islands—San Cristóbal, Floreana, Isabela, and Santiago—though the *Beagle* sailed close enough to give him a good look at eight other islands.

"The natural history of these islands is eminently curious and well deserves attention," he wrote—a much-quoted understatement. Darwin made notes on different creatures and collected specimens. He went on long hikes and took rides on the backs of tortoises. In the highlands of Floreana he was refreshed by the sight of green and thriving vegetation and cool black mud. He also visited a settlement there. On Isabela he scaled a tuff cone (a type of small volcano) and climbed down into its crater to ease his thirst with a drink from a small lake, only to discover that the water was saltier than seawater. He traced tortoises and timed their lumbering pace (well under a quarter-of-a-mile per hour). Land iguanas scurried clumsily out of his way. He opened the stomachs of a few to find out what they ate.

One day he visited with the vice-governor of the islands, Nicholas Lawson (an Englishman serving under Ecuadorian authority), who pointed out that the different islands were inhabited by different varieties of tortoises. For instance, Lawson claimed he could "with certainty" identify which island any particular tortoise inhabited. Though somewhat overstated, this claim was a potentially stunning hint, as Sulloway points out, but Darwin failed to catch its full meaning.

"I did not for some time pay sufficient attention to this statement," Darwin wrote later. "I had already partially mingled together the collections from two of the islands. I never dreamed that islands, about fifty or sixty miles apart, and most of them in sight of each other, formed of precisely the same rocks, placed under a quite similar climate, rising to a nearly equal height, would have been differently tenanted."

Thinking about it after he left the islands, Darwin called it a "remarkable fact" and may have sensed the implications. Discussing Galápagos mockingbirds he wrote that if interisland differences meant that new species had arisen, such a fact would *"undermine the stability of Species."* He was toying with a very big idea—species changing their forms to adapt to local environments—but he was not ready to come to grips with it. Darwin let the idea rest, dismissing the differences

● *An illustration in the 1845 edition of Darwin's* Journal of Researches *compared the beak sizes of four species of Galápagos finches, now commonly known as Darwin's finches: 1) Large Ground Finch, 2) Medium Ground Finch, 3) Small Tree Finch, and 4) Warbler Finch. It was only after the* Beagle *returned to England that Darwin realized the full significance of what he had seen and collected during nineteen days ashore in the Galápagos.*

among mockingbirds and other island organisms as varieties within species. Just as some people have big noses and others have small noses, some birds have thick beaks and some have delicate ones—these are only varieties, not divergences between distinct species.

When the *Beagle* returned to England on 2 October 1836, Darwin got down to the business of working on his journal. His specimens were parcelled out among several institutions, including the British Museum, the Royal College of Surgeons, and the Zoological Society of London.

According to Sulloway, Darwin's conversion to the theory of evolution took place in the second week of March 1837, after he had moved to London and begun to work on his specimens with the prominent ornithologist, John Gould, at the Zoological Society. Gould had access to extensive museum collections and knew far more about South American birds than Darwin. He analyzed Darwin's spec-

● *The summit rim of Volcan Darwin, Isabela, appears across the narrow channel from Fernandina. The volcanic history of these two islands fascinated Darwin. In a journal entry he describes how "immense deluges of black, naked lava . . . have flowed either over the rims of the great caldrons, like pitch over the rim of a pot in which it has been boiled, or have burst forth from smaller orifices on the flanks. In their descent they have spread over miles of the sea-coast." On Isabela, the Beagle crew witnessed "a small jet of smoke curling from the summit of one of the great craters."*

imens, and his report must have come as an astonishing surprise. He pointed out numerous errors in Darwin's tentative voyage classifications. Birds that Darwin had initially identified as a wren and blackbird were actually finches, part of a unique genus within which Gould recognized thirteen species (Gould's thirteen species do not correspond exactly with the thirteen species of Galápagos finches recognized today). Darwin learned that all except one of the land birds he had collected in the Galápagos were endemic—that is, *found only* in the Galápagos Islands—although they were related to South American birds. Finally, said Gould, different species of mockingbirds lived on different islands of the Galápagos—the fact that Darwin had already said would "undermine the stability of Species."

Darwin, scribbling notes on Gould's comments (the notes can still be seen at Cambridge University Library), may have felt the earth shaking already. This bit of evidence, taken in conjunction with the observations and experiences he had gleaned during the *Beagle's* five-year voyage, convinced him that the "species barrier" had been broken. In Darwin's mind, creationist doctrine crumbled. He became an evolutionist.

A scientist with a similar experience today might be tempted to publish the results of research as quickly as possible. Darwin, who of course was a creature of a different time, spent twenty-two years studying aspects of evolution and compiling a great fund of evidence before publishing his findings in 1859 in *On the Origin of Species.*

Not long after his work with Gould, Darwin moved his family from London to the country village of Downe, 16 miles southeast of the capital, where he lived and worked in his large, roomy house called Down House (the village has an "e," the house does not). Between the return of the *Beagle* and his death more than forty-five years of painstaking science intervened.

These years were painful as well as painstaking because of the poor health that afflicted Darwin from his thirties on. Possibly because of an insect bite in South America that may have infected him with a tropical disease, he suffered from nausea, flatulence, and weakness. Often he could not work at his desk for more than twenty minutes without retreating to his couch to rest, yet he wrote fourteen books. It was as if he had used up most of his lifetime allotment of physical vigor in his five years of world travel on the *Beagle*: he never left England again, and he seldom ventured far from Down House. While there are no doubts that he was ill, there are also veiled hints that his seclusion was in part a way of warding off visitors and distractions. It was as if Darwin sensed that the revolution he was to engineer would require a sequestered existence.

Substantial family money erased all financial concerns from his life. He was a "gentleman scholar" and therefore not dependent on

Zenaida Galapagoensis

● *In the third part of the* Zoology of the Voyage of H.M.S. Beagle, *the noted ornithologist John Gould described and illustrated the many bird specimens collected on the Bea-gle voyage, including the beautiful Galápagos Dove. Gould's surprising findings spurred Darwin to the insight that some birds had evolved into distinct new species in adapting to diverse island settings.*

science for his livelihood. Aside from his grief over the death in infancy of three of his eight children and the tribulations of his illness, Darwin's life was tranquil and his time was his own.

He worked with a diligence and patience that seem incredible by any standard. The history of the twenty-two year gestation of *On the Origin of Species* is interesting in itself. Darwin had sketched out the theory in a 35-page draft written in 1842 and with more detail in a 231-page draft in 1844, but obviously neither draft contained the published edition's voluminous evidence, well-ordered arguments, and the extensive discussion of objections he knew would be raised.

"At last gleams of light have come," he wrote in 1844. "I am almost convinced (quite contrary to the opinion I started with) that species are not (it is like confessing a murder) immutable." He knew he would be treated like a murderer of belief, and he did not relish the fury and vilification that would surely descend on his peaceful life in the country.

His tempered pace worked to his advantage when *On the Origin of Species* was finally published fifteen years later. Instead of announcing his findings with all the passion of a new idea, he acted with the sureness of someone whose thinking had matured in a lengthy, rigorous examination. He was circumspect and cautious: he did not expressly debunk all aspects of creationist doctrine (he was willing to admit the creations of one or a few primordial forms) or say much on the explosive subject of man's place in the evolutionary scheme (twelve years would elapse before he launched his thoughts on the shared ancestry of man and ape in *The Descent of Man*). Beyond his caution, his attitude of openness to new information or insights, including those that might require alterations in his theory, probably deflated some of the antagonism of his critics.

Darwin's massive evidence could not be dismissed—this was much more than theorizing. He also had, by this time, won the support of several eminent scientists, friends, and colleagues who had been exchanging opinions on evolution with him throughout the 1840s and 1850s. Another detail that seems to confirm the perfect luck and timing of the 1859 publication was that the review of *On the Origin of Species*—published in Britain's most prestigious journal, *The Times*—fell into the hands of Thomas Henry Huxley. Huxley, a colleague who originally dissented from Darwin's thinking but was on his way to becoming Darwin's most fiery champion, welcomed the book with high and convincing praise. He later remarked that his first reaction on reading *On the Origin of Species* was "How extremely stupid not to have thought of that."

A major spur to Darwin's tortoise-paced approach to publishing was an incident in 1858 involving a younger scientist named Alfred

MAN·IS·BVT·A·WORM.

● *The debate over Darwin's theories often took the form of caricature. "Man Is But a Worm," a Punch cartoon that appeared shortly after the publication of* The Descent of Man *in 1871, made light of Darwin's argument that man too was part of the evolutionary process.*

● *Darwin's "new" study, preserved as it might have looked in Darwin's time, is today part of the Charles Darwin Museum, Down House. In forty years at Down House, Darwin wrote fourteen books, including* On the Origin of Species *and* The Descent of Man.

Russel Wallace. Several years earlier Wallace had come close enough to Darwin's theory to cause alarm among Darwin's friends. Darwin was urged to complete his manuscript rather than risk having his ideas anticipated by someone else. But Darwin was distressed by the unseemly and disruptive prospect of a race with Wallace. He admitted he didn't want to come in second, but he was even more reluctant to abandon his intention of developing evidence in support of every detail.

For a while, neither man did much in terms of scientific competition. Both had taken the huge first step of recognizing that species had been developing continuously by evolution rather than all at once and in final form by divine creation. It was the second great step that slowed things down. If nature, not God, governed the origin of species, what was the law or mechanism that made the process work? The answer would be the solution to the "mystery of mysteries."

Darwin had the answer; he had had it since 1838 but was not finished mulling it over and proving it. The idea of natural selection had occurred to him in his studies of domesticated animals, some of which he encountered and observed in his daily walks at Down House. Then a reading of Thomas Malthus's *Essay on the Principle of Population* led him to wonder about the limits on population caused mainly by the availability of food. If survival of individuals depended on which individuals were best adapted to compete for the food, then variations that provided an advantage probably led to survival, while the disadvantaged individual would ultimately perish.

Variation occurs in all forms of nature. No two individuals are exactly alike and many differences are inheritable. Darwin knew from animal husbandry that certain characteristics could be accentuated or diminished. When pigeons or sheep were modified in this manner, it was called artificial selection. Darwin argued that it also happened naturally. Favorable variations would be selected by nature as permanent features of evolving species. The result was not necessarily a "higher" species but a species that was better adapted to its local environment. Another, more popular name for the process, "survival of the fittest," was coined by the philosopher Herbert Spencer, borrowed by Wallace, and adopted by Darwin in the fifth edition of *On the Origin of Species*, published in 1869.

Who, then, was the man who anticipated Darwin? Alfred Russel Wallace was doing fieldwork on the "species question" in what is now Indonesia when he fell ill with malaria in 1858. In and out of delirium, he too thought of Malthus—and that thought led him directly and independently to the idea of natural selection. It seems amazingly coincidental that one of the people who greatly influenced Malthus was Darwin's grandfather, Erasmus.

Wallace recorded his flash of insight in a short manuscript that he mailed to none other than Charles Darwin. Wallace respected Darwin and asked him to deal with it as he thought best. Some scientists in this position, finding the culmination of twenty years of work equalled by a rival in a malarial delirium might have dealt with it by lighting a fire and throwing the manuscript in. But Darwin said he would rather burn his own book than behave in a "paltry spirit."

The affair was resolved with gentlemanly grace. The findings of the two men were announced simultaneously before a meeting of the distinguished Linnaean Society on 1 July 1858. Darwin could not attend because of the death of his son and an outbreak of disease in his household, and Wallace was far away in the Malay Archipelago. The readings from Wallace and Darwin received little notice and had little immediate impact. The timing and staging apparently were just not right for a revolution to commence.

However, the incident caused Darwin to begin writing in earnest. *On the Origin of Species* was published a year and a half later. This time it had the profound impact that is often described as earth-shaking.

Darwin said later that if Wallace had not prompted him to write, it would have been many more years until he was ready to publish and his book would have been four or five times longer and more difficult to read. Nevertheless, many readers have found the book to be slow-going, especially in contrast to the liveliness of *The Voyage of the Beagle*.

When Darwin died in 1882 his desire to be buried humbly on the grounds of Down House was brushed aside. He was instead buried in the place of highest honor, Westminster Abbey. At his funeral a special anthem was sung in tribute to the man whose dedication and genius had transformed modern thought.

To many people it seems almost a miracle that most of the specimens brought back by Darwin and his *Beagle* shipmates are still intact and available for scientific study. They are kept at the British Museum (Natural History) in London, the British Museum's ornithological collection at Tring (25 miles northwest of London), the University Museum of Zoology in Cambridge, the Rijksmuseum van Natuurlijke Histoire in Leiden, Holland, and elsewhere.

Darwin's specimens have survived because of the arsenic paste that had come into use as a preservative of animal tissue not long before the voyage of the *Beagle*. The technique was a major breakthrough at a time when mapping and collecting expeditions were booming and naturalists on voyages to all parts of the globe were shipping home specimens by the caseload. Unfortunately, the lack of an effective preservative caused the majority of collected specimens, including most of those gathered a half century before Darwin during the famous voyages of Captain James Cook, to decompose even before scientists back in Europe had a chance to look at them.

After taking a specimen, usually by killing it with pepper shot fired from a shotgun, Darwin would slit it open, skin it in a manner that preserves the skull and bones of the wings and legs, and brush the skin with arsenic paste. As in embalming or mummifying, the paste would fix the tissue.

The arsenic would not only preserve tissue without discoloring it, but, since it is a poison, it also made the tissue less appetizing to insect pests that often haunt museum collections. It also prevented the growth of mold and mildew when the specimens were stored in a ship's hold, although it was never safe or pleasant to work with because of its toxic fumes and because it may be assimilated through the skin.

In 1979 and 1985 I went to England to compare fossils I had found in the Galápagos with specimens collected by Darwin 150 years earlier. When you study his specimens and observe his craftsmanship, Charles Darwin seems less of an immortal and much more of a real, hardworking scientist. The continuity of science itself seems dramatic and inspirational when you consider the generations of scientists and curators who have examined the Darwin specimens, including the great ornithologist John Gould, whose comments on these very specimens were instrumental in turning Darwin into an evolutionist. Certainly my own research—as I'll explain in the next chapter—would have been different if the *Beagle* specimens were no longer available for study and comparison.

● *The ornithological branch of the British Museum (Natural History), located in the village of Tring, is the principal repository for bird specimens collected on the* Beagle *voyage.*

Beneath the Surface

The practice of science has some parallels with a detective trying to solve a murder. Both the scientist and the sleuth collect fragments of information they hope will serve as clues, pointing the way to larger revelations. Both try to piece together step-by-step progressions of past events, searching for the body, if it is missing, or at least for its remains. There is often a prime suspect but he is considered only the "alleged perpetrator" until the evidence is conclusive. Finally the homicide detective and the scientist have this in common: they are experts in extinction.

Extinction is part of the ongoing evolutionary process, yet there is no internal mechanism that brings about a species' demise. Neither self-induced nor a consequence of genetic inferiority, extinction is caused by external forces such as changes in climate, habitat, or predation. The more rapidly and drastically such changes occur, the more likely certain species will find themselves unable to cope. As Darwin put it, "The death of a species is a consequence of non-adaptation."

It is well known that animals on islands tend to be more vulnerable to extinction than continental forms. Small population sizes and low levels of immunity to disease can mean the loss of whole species. Island species also tend to be overwhelmed by the arrival of predators—they may be easy victims for the aggressive newcomers. Above all they are vulnerable to the worst fate that can befall an island ecosystem: the coming of man.

Memory of extinct species seldom survives them; the only evidence of their existence is interred with their bones. Though in certain Polynesian islands natives can describe vanished species of the past (usually birds) based on stories passed down over generations, there is little such oral record in the sparsely and recently settled Galápagos, and the chronology of species can only be documented through fossils. Thanks to the geological setting of these islands, much fossil evidence survives and is waiting to be found. In collecting fossils to reconstruct faunal evolution, the scientist must bear in mind that each species and each island has its own history. These histories weave

together and break apart, they shift in and out of focus, and there are countless gaps and ambiguities; the analogy with detective work is not farfetched.

I mentioned in the previous chapter that Storrs Olson, a curator of birds at the Smithsonian's National Museum of Natural History, opened my eyes to the research potential of islands. When Olson and I met in 1976, I was a 25-year-old research assistant and he was 32— young for a mentor—but he had done considerable work with ornithological fossils on islands, especially Hawaii and the South Atlantic islands of Ascension and St. Helena. Our lengthy discussions about other island sites for fossil-gathering research eventually pointed me toward the Galápagos.

It happened that S. Dillon Ripley, the energetic figure who presided over the affairs of the Smithsonian for two decades, was also an ornithologist and one who had a long-standing interest in the Galápagos. Ripley's involvement dated back as far as 1937, when he first visited the islands by boat. In 1958 he took part in an international meeting of scientists that laid much of the groundwork for the national park that was created to preserve the Galápagos a few years later. The Smithsonian became a regular contributor to the Galápagos National Park and to the Charles Darwin Research Station and over the years has consistently contributed to Galápagos conservation efforts.

In 1977 Ripley revisited the islands, and before long it became known that he hoped to increase the Smithsonian's participation in Galápagos research. Ripley approached Olson for suggestions, and Olson nominated me as a ready and willing scientist. The necessary funds were found, and on 3 January 1978, feeling very lucky and a little bit intimidated, I arrived in the islands.

The idea of looking for fossils in young volcanic islands was still new at the time, and some researchers thought digging in the Galápagos would turn up little evidence; after all, such islands lack the fine-grained stratified rocks that typically yield fossils on continents. However, Storrs Olson had already come up with encouraging fossil finds in a variety of settings on other archipelagos and particularly in volcanic caves known as lava tubes. The lava tubes of the Galápagos had been mentioned as early as 1835 by Darwin himself—"the tops of caverns . . . have fallen in, leaving circular pits with deep sides." In 1978 most of them were still unmapped, unexplored, and virtually unknown to science.

The limited purpose of my first trip to the Galápagos was to scout the territory and make preparations for a major fossil-hunting expedition. While taking a solitary walk on the grounds of the Darwin Station, however, I stopped to look into an earthquake crevice about 100 yards from the tortoise pens and tourist area of the Darwin Sta-

● *The Tahiti Black Rail* (Gallirallus pacificus) *is one of countless examples of the acute vulnerability of island species. Known only from this painting by an artist on Captain James Cook's famous expedition of 1773, the Tahiti Black Rail became extinct shortly after Cook's visit. Like many other species of flightless rails in Polynesia, it was unable to cope with the enormous changes introduced by man.*

Preceding page, a land iguana pauses in the sun at the top of Fernandina's single massive volcano. An eruption in 1968 caused the oval-shaped caldera floor to sink 1,200 feet to its present depth of nearly 4,000 feet.

tion. The crevice was about 4 feet wide and 20 feet deep and was partly filled with brackish water.

Beginner's luck must have been with me when I suddenly noticed hundreds of small bones in the dusty, powdery sediment that had accumulated on ledges inside the crevice. The bones were easily recognizable as those of rodents. Screening the sediment back at the Darwin Station, I realized I had found fossils of a prehistorically extinct species, the Santa Cruz giant rat.

What I had found was evidence of a creature that no man ever recorded seeing, including the early explorers, although I suspect it died out less than two hundred years ago. Three bones of this species had been found in 1964 but were incorrectly classified. Clayton Ray, a curator of vertebrate paleontology at the Smithsonian, and I later reclassified this species and outlined its evolutionary link with mainland rodents.

In the next few days, working in the same site, I found hundreds of other bones of the Santa Cruz giant rat and also the bones of two other extinct species: the large Santa Cruz rice rat and the small Santa Cruz rice rat. It seems incredible that the fossils in the Darwin Station earthquake crevice were found so easily—almost in plain sight of a

● *Dark lava flows streak the slopes of one of Isabela's six massive volcanoes. Near the shore, a small vent has erupted to form a typically steep-sided "spatter cone." The Galápagos archipelago ranks with the Hawaiian Islands as a fascinating natural laboratory for the study of oceanic volcanoes. Beneath the surface, subterranean lava tubes— commonly 15 or more feet in diameter and hundreds of feet in length—compel the interest of both paleontologists and geologists because of the rich fossil record they preserve.*

bypasser. Usually it takes a lot more effort and exploration. Indeed, on other trips I have spent as much time searching *for* caves as *within* them for fossils to unearth.

Lava tubes form during the volcanic eruptions that created and continue to enlarge the Galápagos. They begin as passages within a lava flow, where molten lava rushes beneath the surface in tunnels of liquid fire. As the flow of lava subsides, the hotter, thinner lava drains out, leaving a hollow corridor or tube as much as a mile long. On Santa Cruz there are lava tubes so large a bus could drive through them; others are barely big enough for a person to squeeze into. Unlike the deep and labyrinthine passages of limestone caves, lava tubes typically consist of a single chamber just below the surface that runs down slope following the contour of the land.

To enter a lava tube is to find yourself in a place of strange and stark beauty. It is also a place of death and a cemetery for creatures that lived long ago or very recently. A lava tube is a natural trap; its roof, after decades, centuries, or millennia of being weakened by soil formation, root growth, and erosion, eventually collapses under its own weight, falling in and creating an open hole. Then animals stumble in —tortoises, land iguanas, rats. Unable to climb out, they die in the tubes, leaving their remains, which become fossils. (I use the term "fossil" to mean any physical evidence of past life, mineralized or not.)

However, the richest fossil accumulations in the cave are caused by another factor, and for this we must thank the Galápagos Barn Owl for its copious contribution to science. The prey of owls is eaten whole or in large chunks; the soft parts are digested while the bony parts are regurgitated in the form of a shiny, compact pellet about the size of a walnut. If the prey is a reptile, the pellet consists of bones and scales. If it is a bird, bones and feathers predominate. A mammalian pellet is made of bones and fur.

The Galápagos Barn Owl often roosts and nests on ledges in caves. An owl family might live for many generations on the same ledge, producing accumulations of bones that represent the thousands of creatures the owls have eaten over the years. The scales, feathers, and fur of the pellets usually decay with time; however, in dry caves where little mold is growing, the bones do not decay but slowly mineralize and form fossil deposits. Seeking ancient owl vomit sounds like a strange vocation, but to paleontologists these fossilized remains offer valuable evidence of past life.

Exploring a cave we keep a sharp eye out for fossils lying on the floor. Using powerful lights and often working on our hands and knees, we scour the floor for tiny bones of lizards, rodents, and small birds. If we spot fossils on the surface, we make a map of the cave's floor to record the location of the find. Next we search for dry, rather fine-grained sediments in which fossils might be preserved. Finding

such sediment, which might look like sand or fine gravel, we use hand trowels to dig a test pit to sample the fossil content of the strata, removing the sediment in designated levels, usually of 10 centimeters each. This gives us a profile of the deposit and allows us to assess changes in the sediment or in the number and kind of fossils it contains.

Finding significant fossils in a test pit sample is a hint to study the walls of the test pit for changes in color, texture, or anything else that might indicate a promising fossil deposit. Then the test pit is enlarged, following the natural contours of the sediment. After double-checking maps and field notes, the completed excavations are lined with plastic sheeting and filled with rubble to preserve them for future studies by myself or other scientists.

Outside the cave, usually later the same day, the sediment is sifted through mesh screens (window screens, the same kind that keeps the bugs away), leaving us with tiny fossil bones. Newly unearthed fossils are then taken to the Darwin Research Station for preliminary sorting and packaging in cigar boxes lined with cotton and toilet paper. The boxes are sent to the Natural History Museum of the Smithsonian. Their arrival begins a long process of cleaning, sorting, cataloging, identifying, describing, and photographing. When the analysis of a batch of fossils is completed, results are published and a small representative collection is sent back to the Darwin Station for display and study at the Station's Van Straelen Museum. The entire process can take years.

I have found fossils in lava tubes on five Galápagos islands—Santa Cruz, Isabela, Floreana, Rábida, and San Cristóbal. In revealing the existence of extinct species or species no longer found on a particular island, fossils are absolutely essential. For example, fossils I have collected have proved the past existence of Wedge-tailed Shearwaters on San Cristóbal; Galápagos Barn Owls on Floreana; giant rats on Santa Cruz; leaf-toed geckos, land iguanas, and rice rats on Rábida; and giant rats and two species of rice rats on Isabela.

In some of these cases the identification was not immediate but came much later in the lab. For example, on Floreana in 1978 and 1980 I was finding fossilized bones that seemed to have been regurgitated by Galápagos Barn Owls, but Barn Owls had never been found on Floreana, either living or as fossils. It was a mystery until 1981 when, back in Washington, I was studying a batch of my fossils and identified a few fragmentary bones of Barn Owls, proving that in prehistoric times they had indeed been alive and well and regurgitating on Floreana.

In addition, I have found fossils of other species on islands where they were recorded alive by Darwin or other scientists of the nineteenth or early twentieth century but are now extinct. They include:

● *A branch over the mouth of André's Cave, Santa Cruz, supports David Steadman as he descends 20 feet by rope. André's Cave has yielded the finest specimens of the Santa Cruz Giant Rat, a prehistorically extinct species known only from its bones. An entire skeleton, from skull to tail, bottom, was found lying on the surface of the cave floor.*

Opposite, Galápagos Barn Owl— See plate 39.

rice rats and Large Ground Finches from San Cristóbal; Floreana Mockingbirds, Sharp-beaked Ground Finches, Large Ground Finches, snakes and tortoises from Floreana; Sharp-beaked Ground Finches and two species of rice rats from Santa Cruz; and tortoises from Rábida.

Nothing triggers a detective's instincts as much as this kind of physical evidence—fossils showing that numerous species became extinct relatively suddenly, recently, and at about the same time. Assessing what the evidence means, however, requires careful analysis and comparison with earlier findings. Here the *Beagle* specimens stored at Tring, the ornithological branch of the British Museum (Natural History), have offered an indispensable comparative tool.

Darwin's specimens form the starting point in a long-term historical record that researchers can refine with new findings, new methods, new viewpoints and, of course, new disputes. This historical dimension reflects science at its best—like evolution, a continuing process of change in which every ending is also a beginning and every answer can open new questions. Many of the questions raised by Darwin's specimens have been answered only recently by the Darwin scholar, Frank Sulloway, whose work has been so important to my research on the islands.

Working most recently at Harvard, Sulloway is more a historian of science than a biologist, and he has brought the advantage of a fresh perspective to a long-standing debate about Darwin's specimens. I think of him as the principal sleuth who among other things solved the muddle surrounding Darwin's specimen labels.

Darwin's mislabeling was not a matter of carelessness but what might be termed an understandable misunderstanding. When he explored the islands, he still regarded all Galápagos creatures as part of the same divine creation and did not grasp the evolutionary significance of island-to-island differences in species. Therefore on most of his labels he neglected to note the name of the island on which specimens were taken (although occasionally locality details were recorded as incidental information).

Another complication—this time a helpful one—was that Darwin was not the only collector from the *Beagle*. His assistant Syms Covington, Captain FitzRoy himself, and at least two other *Beagle* shipmates, Harry Fuller and Benjamin Bynoe, also gathered specimens. The labels by FitzRoy, Fuller, and Bynoe *did* include island localities, and Darwin referred to these specimens later when he tried through memory and deduction to determine which islands his many specimens had come from.

Complicating matters still further, the British Museum committed what is now regarded as a major curatorial error by snipping off the original field tags, replacing them with standard museum labels. This was a common museological practice at the time, but the curators who made the new labels resolved discrepancies in locality information by choosing Darwin's reconstructed guesses over the more accurate and original notations of the other collectors. Obviously they attached less credibility to nonscientists already fading into history than to Darwin, who had attained considerable scientific stature by the time the British Museum affixed the new labels sometime after 1855. In other instances these curators attached island localities to Darwin's unlabeled specimens which Darwin had derived from other collections and then published. Of course the chance of such a label being correct was once in four (the number of islands on which Darwin collected specimens).

In clipping the field tags, the curators lost not only accurate information on the non-Darwin specimens but also the question marks Darwin had written on tags he was not sure about. Thus in addition to introducing mistakes, the curators erased all hints of doubt. Many years went by before the *Beagle* labels were questioned; to do so, of course, was to question not only a venerated scientist, but one particularly known for his meticulousness.

Researchers on most subsequent Galápagos expeditions, notably the large-scale expedition by the California Academy of Sciences in 1905–1906, were familiar with the complexities of evolutionary theory. Alert to the importance of island-by-island differences, they carefully labeled specimens according to the individual islands from which they were taken. When such specimens were compared with Darwin's specimens, however, bewildering discrepancies—a veritable "taxonomic nightmare" to use Sulloway's term—emerged. Ornithologists even tried to reconcile the problems by assuming that some species in the *Beagle* collection had evolved in size and shape in the short period of time since Darwin first collected them.

The consequence was that a few decades of confidence in Darwin's labels were followed by nearly a century of uncertainty. The *Beagle* labels were so disputed that the accuracy of past and present work was also jeopardized. Scientists blamed the confusion on the removal of the field tags; they were not even aware of the earlier complications resulting from Darwin's mislabeling. Meanwhile, time was wasted on wrong directions and speculation.

The controversy continued until Sulloway undertook a detailed investigation of all the *Beagle* collections in the late 1970s. While he dug into the history of the specimens, I was digging in the lava tubes of the Galápagos. Though we were unknown to each other at the time, we were soon coming up with mutually corroborating results.

This brings us to the case of a bird called the Large Ground Finch. On Floreana Island, according to the museum's label, Darwin and others from the *Beagle* collected eight specimens of this bird. But when the California Academy researchers visited Floreana, they found no traces of the Large Ground Finch. Was the label incorrect, or was

● *At the Charles Darwin Research Station, David Steadman washes sediment through ¹/₁₆″ mesh screens. Screening or "sieving" samplings is the first step in a long process of specimen analysis. Fossils are then sorted and labelled, bottom, before being shipped to the Smithsonian.*

there some other explanation? It was suggested that a Large Ground Finch never existed on Floreana and that the *Beagle* specimens were taken on Santiago Island where a very similar but smaller race of Large Ground Finch exists today. Perhaps the Large Ground Finch had undergone an "evolutionary shrinkage" on Santiago in the extraordinarily short period between 1835 and 1905.

Sulloway's research, however, convinced him that the Floreana labels were correct. Meanwhile I was underground in Floreana finding bones of a big finch—not only finding these bones but finding them in large quantities. It was clear that a bird that was no longer to be found had once been quite common.

I packed my finch fossils from Floreana and went to the British Museum to compare them with Large Ground Finches collected by the *Beagle*. I measured Darwin's specimens (every scientist takes his own measurements, which usually differ from what other scientists have found) and took X-rays of them. The comparisons showed that my fossils and the *Beagle* specimens were a perfect match. Looking at these aged and historic specimens, the only modern physical remnants of this species, I finally saw the bird I had known only by its bones. The comparison proved that Darwin's birds *were* from Floreana and the shrunken finch theory was wrong.

The analysis also proved that a species that existed in 1835 (and was common then, to judge from Darwin's collection from Floreana) had become extinct by 1905. Indeed there had been Galápagos expeditions of smaller scope than the California Academy's at a rate of about one per decade: an 1852 Swedish expedition on Floreana did not find the Large Ground Finch, nor did an 1846 British expedition or a French expedition in 1838 or any other expedition. A common species had virtually ceased to exist in a period that may have been *no longer than a few years.*

Moreover, Sulloway and I had both found compelling evidence of a second murder. In the British Museum collection there was another species that pointed to a drama of quick extinction—the specimens of the rice rat collected by Darwin on the island of San Cristóbal. Like the Large Ground Finch, this rat was never seen again after the *Beagle* sailed away from the Galápagos. It was time to find the culprit.

At this point history came to the aid of science in providing the crucial clue. As noted earlier, the first permanent settlement in the Galápagos was an Ecuadorian penal colony established in 1832 on Floreana. Three hundred political prisoners and their jailers had arrived to share the island with, among other creatures, the Large Ground Finch. Now here was an unmistakable lead. The human colonists had brought with them a selection of domestic animals from the mainland—cats, dogs, horses, cattle, goats, donkeys, and (inadvertently)

● *These seven specimens of Large Ground Finch—now part of the British Museum (Natural History) ornithological collection—were collected by Darwin and other members of the* Beagle *crew on Floreana and San Cristóbal. Within a few decades of Darwin's visit, the Large Ground Finch had vanished from these two islands.*

rats. Clearly these introduced species might be responsible for the Large Ground Finch's demise, but the hypothesis raised another question: why was the Large Ground Finch extinguished while other creatures, including other finches, survived?

Cactus may be the key. The introduced domestic animals quickly became wild, and, roaming the parched Floreana lowlands in search of water, they discovered that the prickly pear cactus was a good water source. Goats and donkeys learned to knock the cactus down and mash it open to extract the moisture.

The Large Ground Finch had a massive beak, an indication that it was specialized to eat large seeds, and the Floreana prickly pear cactus (which barely exists today) had the biggest seeds of any Galápagos cactus. The Large Ground Finch fed on these seeds and nested among the plant's thorny pads, whereas other finches were less specialized feeders and nesters. Only a few years after the penal colony had been established, there were probably not enough cacti left to support the Large Ground Finch, and it died out.

What about the San Cristóbal rice rat? In the mid-1840s the penal colony was moved from Floreana to San Cristóbal, taking along its animal population, including the infamous black rat. The rice rat was simply unable to coexist with the aggressive black rat and disappeared completely, perhaps from a disease transmitted by the black rats.

Sulloway's sleuthing in the case of the Large Ground Finch and other species was the first breakthrough in the labeling confusion and at last straightened out which labels were credible and which were not. He also exposed some of the flaws in the nearly mythic legend of Darwin in the Galápagos.

That legend says simply that Darwin looked on the drab sparrow-sized finches of the Galápagos and, noting the diversity in the form and function of their beaks, at once understood how a species could branch off in divergent directions in the process of adaptation and natural selection. There were beaks for crushing big seeds, beaks for eating small soft seeds, and beaks for eating insects. Other adaptations included a vegetarian finch and a warblerlike finch with a small, thin beak. Perhaps the most fascinating is the Woodpecker Finch, a species unknown to Darwin that often holds thorns or small twigs in its beak to probe in wood for insects.

The appeal of the finch story lies in its schoolbook clarity and simplicity. Rather than competing for the same limited food supply, the finches had diversified by filling niches in nature normally occupied by other birds. For example, a finch that specialized in big seeds was not competitive with a finch that ate small seeds. And the various insect-eating finches certainly did not compete for food with the seed-eating species. Even among themselves, the insect-eating finches were pursuing their prey with different beaks and different habits.

The number of Galápagos finch species is given as thirteen, and for years the topic of evolution has typically been introduced to high school biology students through an illustration showing these species arrayed in profile, contrasting the differences in their beaks. A form of this illustration appeared in 1947 in the famous book *Darwin's Finches*, by David Lack, a British ornithologist who devoted much of his career to studying the birds. Indeed, it was largely owing to Lack's book that the birds became known as Darwin's finches, rather than by their collective name, Galápagos finches.

David Lack was an excellent scientist, but he confined his studies mainly to the observation of living birds. In order to classify the finches, his priority was to pigeonhole them into species, based mainly on their beaks and the various feeding habits they represented. He came up with the currently accepted number of species, thirteen, deemphasizing the role of many intermediate hybrids and the insights they offer into the question of ancestry.

The aura of Darwin's name and their neatness as an evolutionary example so elevated the finches that they were regarded as instrumental in Darwin's formulation of evolutionary theory. Sulloway showed that this was not true by carefully reviewing all the evidence in its historical context. Common sense alone supports his thesis: if Darwin had seen the finches in a great "Eureka" moment of evolutionary insights, he would have shown far more interest in them while in the Galápagos and certainly would have labeled them correctly.

Sulloway points out that Darwin later became keenly aware of the bumbled labeling and the inadequate attention he had given the finches while in the Galápagos; he took the prudent course, which was to steer clear of them for ten years after the *Beagle*'s return. Then, in the *second* edition of *The Voyage of the Beagle* (1845), Darwin wrote this famous sentence: "Seeing this gradation and diversity of structure in one small, intimately related group of birds, one might really fancy that from an original paucity of birds in this archipelago, one species had been taken and modified for different ends." In Darwin's most important work, *On the Origin of Species*, the finches were not mentioned at all.

If Darwin's personal relation to the finches has been much exaggerated, it is not as if the finches are unimportant to evolutionary theory. In my view, their significance emerges clearly if the focus changes from the *differences* contrasted in Lack's illustration to the *similarities* that point up the dynamics of evolution. Instead of thinking of the evolutionary chart of the finches as a well-developed family tree with clean branches heading off in distinct directions, I find it useful to think of it as a young bush in which branches are so tangled, untrimmed, and interrelated that evolutionary directions remain jumbled and tentative. Darwin evidently appreciated this point, and this

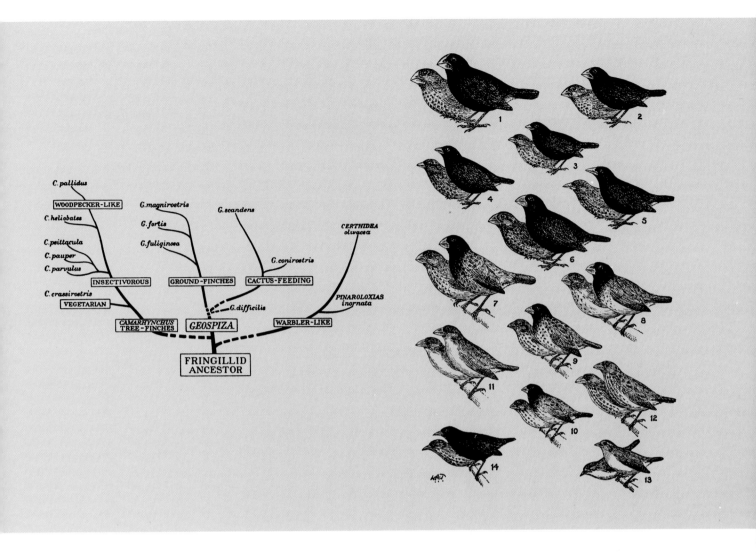

may be part of the reason he did not cite them in the *Origin* as a decisive proof of evolution. The case was just too blurred, too complex, to convince anyone who did not already believe in evolution.

My argument is that while the birds at the most divergent ends of the finch spectrum are indeed distinctly different, the finches in between are emphatically similar; the gradation between them slowly crosses a continuum in which there are no dramatic jumps. Gaps are instead filled by all manner of intermediate forms, blurring all distinctions between any two closely related species.

This is a signal that finches are still in an early stage of evolution called "adaptive radiation." It is as if, like young adults, they are experimenting with different adult identities, some aspects of which they will keep and some they will discard. The experimentation is reflected in the diversity of hybrids, which are produced at a much higher rate than that of older, established species. For instance, each

● *Two illustrations from David Lack's book,* Darwin's Finches, *have often been reproduced as textbook cases of the adaptive radiation of species. In some instances, the profiles, right, have been superimposed on the branches of an evolutionary tree, left, suggesting deceptively clear-cut distinctions among the different finches. Lack recognized thirteen species in the Galápagos; no. 14, the Cocos Finch (Geospiza inornata) is confined to Cocos Island, 400 miles northeast of the Galápagos.*

● *Like Darwin's finches, the Hawaiian finches or "honeycreepers" offer a striking example of natural selection in action. The more than 43 known species of honeycreepers have evolved distinct bill sizes and shapes to exploit a variety of food sources. Unfortunately, forest clearing and the introduction of foreign plants, animals, and diseases have caused the extinction of many honeycreepers, including the four species illustrated in this plate from* Rothschild's Extinct Birds.

species of Hawaiian finch—having had several million more years in which to evolve—is perfectly distinct from the next. Earlier in their history, however, the Hawaiian finches probably followed the same sort of tangled evolutionary course that we see today in Darwin's finches.

At this point we are no longer able to avoid a question that exasperates scientists and nonscientists alike in determining distinct species lines: what is it that separates one species from another? Here the real world fails to conform to the designs our organized minds—yearning to categorize, classify, and pigeonhole—would like to impose. Whereas it is easy enough, for example, to classify Great Horned Owls and Screech Owls as separate species, what about this finch versus that finch? What about finches that are far more similar than different?

Darwin himself struggled with this problem; experts on scientific systematics are forever squabbling over specific cases. The basic principle, which sounds much simpler than it really is, is that a species becomes fixed in its definition when it loses the ability to exchange genes with members of other species to which it was formerly related. Physical and behavioral mechanisms guarantee that Great Horned Owls don't exchange genes with Screech Owls, but in the Galápagos finches are still swapping genes with other finches and creating hybrids. Species lines are not yet so sharply defined that interbreeding and hybridization are ruled out.

This is not a sexual free-for-all among finches—they are at a phase where they *usually* mate with their own species. However, because the anatomical and behavioral differences between the finch species are so slight, they often mate with finches regarded as different species. The hybridization rate among Darwin's finches is difficult to calculate with complete accuracy although perhaps as many as 10 percent of the finches interbreed. While these percentages might sound low, they are in fact much higher than among any other birds, confirming high evolutionary activity.

The appeal of the argument for thirteen clear-cut types of finch is obvious (and someday the figure might be correct), but the finch design is still in flux. The point underscores a fundamental aspect of evolution: the current fuzziness in species definitions, chaotic as they may be, emphasizes the energy of evolution as contrasted to the changeless condition of Creationism.

It also illustrates the constant proliferation of new questions. In 100,000 years will there be many more finch species than now or will they consolidate into fewer species? Will the Woodpecker Finch, which has hybridized with Warbler Finches and Small Tree Finches and might still breed with other finches, remain a highly specialized tool-user or will it drift back toward average finchdom?

Scientists will have to endure the lack of definition until the finch situation is sorted out; in the meantime serious fossil study can help to illuminate which directions the finches have taken in their complex evolutionary course. The sheer quantity of fossils will be important because of the need for a large statistical sample: five fossils could never represent the entire finch fauna, whereas five thousand fossils would give a truer picture. Remember too that each island in the Galápagos has its own history of evolution.

The goal of my work with Galápagos fossils is to piece together a more complete faunal history of the islands. Delving into the past has important conservation applications, which I will describe in the next chapter, but it also serves the scientific purpose of amassing pure knowledge—which may or may not have practical uses later on. In attempting to reconstruct the evolutionary history of Darwin's finches, I have been intrigued in particular by one unanswered question: the identity of the original Darwin's finch.

As I have noted, David Lack did not delve into the ancestry of Darwin's finches, nor had other scientists managed to track down the mainland finch that originally colonized the Galápagos. The consensus was that the riddle was unsolvable for two reasons—because the ancestral species was extinct, its record lost forever in the mists of time, and because Darwin's finches were thought to have diverged so much from other finches that points of resemblance would be too hazy to allow any definite conclusions. Further, Darwin's finches were wrapped securely in the triple mystique of Evolution-Darwin-Galápagos. The origin of the finches was a mystery that seemed too sacred to solve.

Sacred to some, but not impenetrable if approached from new angles. In the summer of 1979, while working at the Smithsonian, I took up the ancestry question as a challenging research project. My primary suspect was the Blue-black Grassquit, a finch commonly found throughout Central and South America, including the Pacific coast from Mexico to Chile.

The first clue was the grassquit's plumage, which for males is shiny black with a purplish sheen whereas the female's is brown and streaked. At least seven species of Darwin's finches have the same types of plumage, though somewhat duller—consistent with the flat coloring that is common in the dark volcanic landscape of the Galápagos. Then I compared skulls of the grassquit and all other mainland finches with skulls of Darwin's finches, including the two most "primitive" species: the Small Ground Finch and the Sharp-beaked Ground Finch. The skull of the grassquit perfectly matched my concept of the skull of the ancestral Darwin's finch.

The grassquit is a bit smaller than most Darwin's finches, though its relatively longer wings and tail make it a better flier, one capable of making the flight from the mainland to the Galápagos. Once in the archipelago, it would have developed the reduced wings and tail common among island birds, which often lose their ability for long-distance flying. Despite this small difference in size, the similarities in skeletons and plumage (shared by no other mainland finches), as well as some shared behavioral patterns, convinced me that the Blue-black Grassquit was the long-sought ancestor of Darwin's finches. Not all scientists have agreed with me, but some concur that the Blue-black Grassquit offers a reasonable answer to a perplexing riddle.

The case for the grassquit would be greatly strengthened if a few grassquit fossils, or even a few fossils that are intermediate between grassquits and Darwin's finches, were one day discovered on the islands. Unfortunately, I doubt that this will happen, as the number of Blue-black Grassquits that reached the Galápagos would have been very small and only impossible luck could overcome the statistical odds. Moreover, the lava tubes that were open and collecting bones

● *The Blue-black Grassquit (Geo-spiza jacarina: female, above; male, below) may be the mainland species whose colonization of the Galápagos gave rise to the diversity of Darwin's finches on the islands today.*

74

when the grassquit arrived (perhaps 100,000 or so years ago) have probably eroded and collapsed completely by now, burying these tiny ancient remains under tons of rubble.

Although time is a key element in studying evolution, it is not always easy to determine the age of a fossil deposit. For example, a few years ago I submitted several plant samples from the fabulously rich fossil site of Cueva de Kubler on Santa Cruz Island for dating by radiocarbon. (I have collected some 400,000 fossils from this cave—the most complete faunal sample of any of the Galápagos islands.) Radiocarbon testing determines age by measuring the amount of decay of the radioactive carbon that exists in all organisms. I sent plant material rather than animal bone as it usually dates more accurately.

The results were quite unexpected. The oldest date was 1700 years ago, not especially remarkable. But the youngest sample dated *in the future*—that is, the test found enough radioactive carbon to indicate a death in A.D. 3245!

The explanation lies in radioactive contamination caused by fallout from nuclear weapons testing—from French tests in Polynesia or United States tests in Micronesia in the 1950s. The contamination was carried on the wind for hundreds of miles; a hard rainstorm washed it out of the air and brought it down on a tiny spot on a tiny island. There is no evidence that the radioactive fallout was widespread and indeed most of my other samples were not touched by it. Yet it seems ominous and chilling that the contamination of the modern world should reach into prehistoric caves in this most pristine of places.

● *A pair of finches has woven acacia branches into the intricate tangle of a nest. Though widely divergent in their feeding habits, all species of Darwin's finches build a similar type nest with a characteristic side entrance.*

5

On Friends and Enemies of Species

"A gun here is almost superfluous," Darwin wrote, describing the vulnerability of Galápagos wildlife in *The Voyage of the Beagle*. With the muzzle of his shotgun he pushed a hawk off a branch. With his hat he almost caught a dove. A mockingbird landed on a pitcher and continued sipping the water in it even as Darwin lifted the jug from the ground.

The tameness of resident species makes a deep impression. What has happened, in effect, is that Galápagos creatures have *forgotten* fear. For example, consider the finch, arriving in the islands some 100,000 years ago with a full set of fear instincts. On the mainland it faced perhaps fifty different types of predators, including mammals, reptiles, and other birds. In the Galápagos, it contends with only three—the Galápagos Barn Owl, the Short-eared Owl, and the Galápagos Hawk, all of which prefer to eat rodents and are fairly indifferent to finches. Living in a nearly predator-free environment for generation after generation, the finches (and other species) lost most of their self-protective instincts.

Then man arrived and suddenly the absence of fear became a potentially fatal liability. It was important to re-acquire the ability to respond to predators, but evolution can be an agonizingly slow process. Darwin, citing the writings of earlier explorers in the islands, suggested that Galápagos birds were once even tamer and had probably regained some of their fear instincts, but not enough. He was surprised that the birds' fear of man had not developed more urgently after a century and a half of frequent visits by buccaneers and whalers who took "cruel delight" in abusing wildlife.

Looking at the situation in evolutionary terms, Darwin speculated that a "salutary dread" of man "is not acquired by individual birds in a short time, even when much persecuted: but that in the course of successive generations it becomes hereditary."

Until fear of man again became part of their instinctive equipment, however, the fate of the islands' birds would be predictably heartrending; Darwin seems to shudder as he reflects on it in the last

to excellent leadership, especially by the recently retired park superintendent, Miguel Cifuentes. Faced by pressure and problems from innumerable sources, he strictly enforced the laws and principles of long-term conservation, dealing effectively with residents, scientists, tourists, park wardens, Darwin Station staff, and government officials, as well as outsiders—entrepreneurs, journalists, VIPs, and others—across a sensitive range of nationalities, political viewpoints, and commercial agendas. Such policies are still being implemented today.

In the division of labor between the two organizations, scientists of the Darwin Station give advice and oversight to scientific and conservation projects and the Park Service administrates the park. Wardens of the Park Service carry out such tasks as collecting tortoise eggs so they can be hatched in safety (rather than eaten by predators), shooting feral goats and donkeys, poisoning feral dogs, maintaining trails, monitoring tourism, and keeping a running census of wildlife populations.

Thanks to such activities you can go the Galápagos today and find a healthy ecology. To be sure, problems are never-ending. Farmers and villagers continually press to expand their activity into park land. A feral animal that is eliminated at great effort from one island suddenly appears on another. And so on.

In their zeal to protect wildlife, conservationists have a tendency to overlook people, but the Galápagos program has stressed the importance of making island and mainland Ecuadorians aware of a national stake in the future of the archipelago. There has been an emphasis on conservation education for local school children and tourism is encouraged. Ecuadorians increasingly realize that the islands are a national treasure in themselves, and also as a source of tourist income (Galápagos tourism is popular with Europeans and North Americans as well as South Americans). This revenue helps the government pay the salaries and basic operating costs of the National Park, but it should be remembered that Ecuador is not a rich country and outside financial support for conservation programs will always be necessary.

Part of the impetus for the sudden influx of visitors to the islands was a stunning television film made in the early 1960s called *The Enchanted Isles*. The film set off such a rush of tourists that alarmed authorities sprang into action, establishing rules and regulations that are still in force today. The Park Service designed a system of zones, designating vast areas off-limits to anyone without a good cause, such as scientific research. Certain beaches that could easily be approached by boats and areas of special appeal to the general public were included in zones where tourist parties are permitted.

Today about 88 percent of the archipelago is considered National Park land, and all tours—led by guides trained in a demanding course

● *The Charles Darwin Research Station is the focal point of scientific study in the islands. In addition to the administration building, left, and the library, right, station facilities include laboratories, captive breeding pens, and the Beagle IV, a boat for transporting scientists among the islands.*

given annually by the Park Service and the Darwin Station—are limited in size and restricted to day visits on all but the main islands. The principle of non-interference with nature and the rule of taking nothing but pictures is understood and accepted, and so far tourists have appreciated that such restrictions guarantee the Galápagos will remain the special islands they are. The numbers continue to increase dramatically (in the last decade alone the annual count has doubled, to about eighteen thousand visitors), but it is generally agreed that tourism, while often a negative in other places, is definitely a positive force in the Galápagos.

The threat of human destructiveness to the islands' delicate ecology comes rather from the population of permanent settlers. I want to qualify this statement immediately because many island residents have been positive contributors to conservation activities. It is important, however, to describe some of the negative impact associated with island residents, some of whom settled here decades ago. An extreme example of the kind of damage humans can cause was the 1985 fire on Isabela Island, apparently started by settlers who lit fires to burn brush off their fields. The fire aroused worldwide concern among conservationists and was covered by the international news media. It lasted five months and destroyed about 200 square miles of wilderness. The ecological consequences are still being assessed; they may be disastrous.

Less striking but in many ways more threatening are three other problems associated with residents. First, some settlers become efficient hunters of native animals. They kill for food (tortoises, doves),

● *At Punta Espinosa, Fernandina, a nonchalant group of sea lions mingles with visitors on a Smithsonian-sponsored tour. The extreme tameness of Galápagos species strikes even the most casual visitor to the islands.*

to control predators (hawks, owls), or from aversion (snakes, lizards). These activities are restricted on National Park lands, but settlers know the islands well and often manage to skirt the law.

Second, settlers bring exotic plants, especially food crops like guava, avocados, and citrus trees or alien grasses for cattle. Certain of these plants become wild and begin to compete with native plants.

Third, and by far the most serious problem, settlers often bring pets and farm animals, such as dogs, cats, rats, mice, pigs, goats, cattle, donkeys, horses, and chickens, and to a lesser extent sheep, guinea pigs, and pigeons. Not one of these animals is native to the Galápagos; they are referred to as "introduced species." Sooner or later these domesticated animals escape from the farms and form wild or "feral" populations. It should be noted that of the feral animals of the Galápagos, only dogs are dangerous to people. They often travel in small packs, perhaps five to a group, and can be quite frightening. I have found that a well-aimed sling shot keeps them at a safe distance.

Among the feral animals in the Galápagos, cats and dogs become predators while sheep, cattle, goats, donkeys, and horses damage vegetation. Omnivorous pigs are destructive in both ways, as are black rats. Chickens (and perhaps pigeons) may introduce diseases such as avian pox.

The conservationist frame of mind in the Galápagos is to regard the feral animals not as new citizens with equal ecological rights but as criminal intruders to be pursued without mercy. Unfortunately, these criminals are tough and resourceful. They are also fertile. A male and two female goats were introduced (in more ways than one) on the island of Pinta in 1959; by 1973 the island's goat population had grown from three to thirty thousand, and it was necessary to begin a program of hunting and killing them. That program has now been successfully completed. Of all feral animals, goats have been the most devastating to vegetation. Feral donkeys would be just as destructive but their populations are smaller.

The island of Santiago has 100,000 goats plus 30,000 feral pigs, creating one of the most formidable conservation problems in the archipelago. The pigs, which are hard to kill because of their nocturnal habits, damage plants, cause severe erosion, and eat the eggs and young of tortoises, green turtles, land iguanas, geckos, lava lizards, snakes, and ground-nesting birds.

Feral dogs are the most destructive predators in the islands, feeding heavily on marine and land iguanas. (They have wiped out the last colonies of land iguanas on southern Isabela and northern Santa Cruz.) They also kill marine birds, fur seals, sea lions, and the eggs and young of tortoises. If dogs ever manage to cross the harsh lava isthmus between northern and southern Isabela, they could attack virtually all of the Galápagos' most celebrated species: tortoises, land and

marine iguanas, penguins, flightless cormorants, fur seals, and sea lions. Pets like dogs (and cats, which menace reptiles and birds) quickly become expert hunters. I believe they should be outlawed in the islands.

Black rats have come up a few times in these pages for obvious reasons. Not only are they one of the worst threats to any island eco-system, they may also be the most difficult to eradicate. They exist on seven Galápagos islands, eating both plant material and the eggs of tortoises and birds. They are also held responsible for wiping out most species of Galápagos rice rats, possibly by transmitting a parasite or disease to which the rice rats were not immune, comparable, say, to Europeans introducing measles or smallpox to Polynesia.

So far there is no effective weapon against the black rats. A new nontoxic chemical about three hundred times more bitter than quinine might be used to keep rats at a distance from tortoise nests, but the protective shells of baby tortoises do not harden for several years: as soon as the young tortoises ventured away from the nests, the rats would pounce. In an experiment on Floreana, poisoned bait effectively kept rats away from the nests of the highly endangered marine bird, the Dark-rumped Petrel. However, as soon as the Darwin Station and

● *A school of surgeonfish clusters in a shallow water reef. The spectacular undersea world of the Galápagos has long been overshadowed by the islands' famous terrestrial dwellers. The land and sea ecosystems are so deeply interdependent, however, that the establishment of a marine pre-serve may be the next critical step in the Galápagos conservation effort.*

National Park workers succeeded in warding off the rats, the petrel nests were instead attacked and devastated by feral cats.

Man and the animals he has introduced are not the only enemies of Galápagos species. In my trip to the islands in 1983 I saw what the weather can do, namely the weather condition (often described inadequately as an ocean current) called *El Niño*.

El Niño occurs with variable severity and at irregular intervals ranging from one to twelve years, usually beginning around December and continuing until March, but in some cases lasting as long as two years. The weather seems to turn tropical: air temperatures rise, rainfall becomes heavy, and the normally cool ocean waters of the region become abnormally warm.

The El Niño of 1982–83 was the most severe ever recorded. It lasted ten months, from November of 1982 until the following August. The rain was relentless. The southern coast of Santa Cruz, with an average annual rainfall of 10 inches, received 140 inches. The island of Genovesa, which averages 5 inches a year, recorded 95 inches. The island of Santa Fé, which averages a bit over 5 inches a year, received 5 inches in one day.

In coastal Ecuador, the rain caused landslides, mudslides, floods, and crop failures that resulted in death and starvation. Thousands died of typhoid and other diseases and mudslides killed hundreds of people. Railroads and most highways on the steep western slopes of the Andes were shut down and transportation backed up everywhere. The effects of the weather were felt even in Ecuador's capital city of Quito,

• *The 1982–83 El Niño transformed the normally parched and barren lowlands of Floreana into a tropical landscape of rushing streams and thick-growing vines and shrubs.*

which lies 100 miles inland in the valley between the western and eastern ridges of the Andes. My flight into Quito was delayed because planes could not land: the airport was mudded in—a mudslide had covered the runway with a 12-inch layer of mud.

Arriving in the Galápagos for fieldwork, I found the lava tubes wet and slippery and there seemed to be more falls than ever. The cuts and bruises hurt more than usual because nothing was being accomplished; fighting fevers from intestinal infections, I cut short the trip and went home.

El Niño's effect on Galápagos wildlife was mixed: good for some, bad for others. Many sea birds died or simply flew away, their reproduction far below its normal rate because of massive mortality among the fish they feed on. The fish died because the plankton they usually eat could not survive in the overly warm, nutrient-poor waters of El Niño.

Land birds, on the other hand, thrived. For most species of land birds in the Galápagos or coastal Ecuador and Peru, successful nesting depends on significant rainfall, and El Niño's rainfall was drenchingly significant. Galápagos Doves, Dark-billed Cuckoos, Yellow Warblers, and all species of mockingbirds and finches were in the midst of a ten-month reproductive binge. The results were multiple nestings and high rates of success in raising young birds.

The warmth and wetness were good for reptiles and land mammals (lizards, snakes, rodents, and bats) but bad for reptiles and mammals of the sea: marine iguanas, fur seals, and sea lions suffered heavy losses. Unlike the sea birds that left the Galápagos, they lacked the range to go off on long searches for better conditions. For example, a marine iguana whose algal food has been replaced by another species of algae because of abnormally warm sea temperatures will starve rather than swim 500 to 1000 miles to find acceptable grazing.

I saw hundreds of dead or starving marine iguanas during my 1983 trip. Many sea lions were also dead or malnourished because the fish they depend on were so scarce. Reproduction in sea lions and fur seals was nil because the mothers were unable to keep their pups alive. It seemed that all the marine creatures I saw would gladly have been swept away to distant shores; their numbers were down and those that remained alive were starving. Yet while these scenes seem sad and cruel to human eyes, they are part of the natural life cycle of these species, and may even have a balancing rather than an unbalancing effect. As soon as El Niño dissipates and the normal food supply returns, the marine iguanas and sea lions begin to feed, reproduce, and rebuild their populations.

In the Galápagos, the 1982–83 El Niño created conditions that startled everyone who went there, particularly those who went with pre-El Niño images in their minds. Of the thirteen islands I visited,

each was dramatically transformed. Most apparent, even when approaching from a boat, was the lushness of the vegetation. The areas usually known as arid lowlands were bright and varied with greenery. In the normally waterless lowlands of Santa Cruz, Santa Fé, and Floreana, waterfalls cascaded over cliffs and into the sea.

One effect of all the rain was a drastic flushing of terrestrial debris into the ocean, convincingly demonstrating that most dispersal of vegetation between islands was probably caused by seeds being washed off one shore and up on another during severe El Niños of the past. The same might be true for animals.

Until the various physical and biological effects of the 1982–83 El Niño are fully analyzed, there will be no saying for sure whether its extreme effects will have extreme long-term consequences. My strong impression during my visits in 1984 and 1985 was that the imbalances in populations were only temporary and that most species were back to normal. This in turn suggests that nature rebounds smoothly from natural blows; man-inflicted blows can cause far more trouble.

Historically, the first of those man-inflicted blows was directed at the Galápagos tortoise, which is still far from recovered from the decimation of the past two centuries. Several hundred thousand tortoises were taken away, mainly by whalers; I have noted that the tortoise populations became so depleted that by the late nineteenth century ships no longer found it worthwhile to come to the Galápagos to hunt them. (This may have been a reprieve for other species as well.) Human predation on tortoises is now negligible, though it still breaks out in deplorable instances. In 1980 the carcasses of twenty-seven female tortoises were found on Isabela, apparently butchered for food.

Remarkably, eleven of the fifteen subspecies of Galápagos tortoise survived the onslaught of the whalers, though many needed priority assistance by the Darwin Station and National Park. The tortoise sub-

species from Floreana, Santa Fé, Rábida, and Fernandina are either extinct or believed extinct. A fifth subspecies was thought to be extinct until 1972 when wardens, who were working to exterminate the feral goats on Pinta Island, discovered the single male tortoise that is now widely known as Lonesome George.

He is called lonesome because he is apparently the last of his kind. No Pinta females have been found, and so far he has rebuffed females of other subspecies. He is considered to be in his procreative prime with perhaps many decades to live. (The lifespan of Galápagos tortoises is unknown but estimated to be quite long—one hundred years or more.) One possible strategy is to try to mate him with females of the very similiar subspecies that lives on Volcan Wolf (*volcan* is Spanish for volcano) on Isabela. If this were achieved, the tortoise couple and their offspring could be resettled on Pinta, where the potential for future reproduction would be good because the island has no introduced predators or herbivores besides goats, and they have now been almost eradicated.

Lonesome George has become a celebrity, an enduring emblem of the Galápagos conservation effort. He lives in a penned area at the Darwin Station. He is not alone as he has several tortoise friends and receives plenty of attention from staff and tourists who readily identify with his plight. Concepts like the impact of man and the extinction of species seem to take on emotional substance in the plodding form of Lonesome George. There is also the fascination of seeing the *one* survivor, the final punctuation of a race. Here again, the Galápagos provides a living-and-breathing illustration of a moment in evolution.

The most populous concentrations of Galápagos tortoises today feed on the plant life growing on the slopes of three volcanoes on Isabela: Volcan Alcedo (5,000 tortoises) and two active volcanoes, Volcan Darwin (1,000) and Volcan Wolf (1,000). Smaller tortoise populations, numbering in the hundreds, exist on other islands.

The Darwin Station and National Park Service have intervened actively to save tortoise eggs and hatchlings. Eggs from tortoise nests are taken to the Darwin Station for incubation. The hatchlings are raised in captivity until they are five years old, by which time they are sufficiently armored to survive the attacks of predators.

The young tortoises are then returned or "repatriated" to their island of origin. Unfortunately, they soon encounter their old enemies, the dogs, rats, cats, and pigs that prevent their offspring from surviving. Until these aggressive predators are eradicated, tortoises will have to depend on man to survive.

Another emblem of Galápagos wildlife are the islands' iguanas, creatures so exotic-looking that they seem to have come out of prehistory—or at least out of horror comic books. The truth is that they are just large, modern lizards. At some time, perhaps after they colonized

● *Already by the turn of the twentieth century, the Pinta Island race of giant tortoises had been severely reduced by whalers in search of food and turtle oil. Today Lonesome George is the sole survivor of his race.*

the islands, the iguanas diverged into a land-dwelling species and a marine species.

The land iguana has had a harder time surviving since the coming of man. Abundant in Darwin's time, it has suffered from predation. Today it thrives on only three islands, Santa Fé, South Plaza, and Fernandina; Fernandina has the largest and least vulnerable population.

Land iguanas lived somewhat abundantly on Santa Cruz and Isabela until most of them were massacred by dogs in the mid-1970s. Some of the iguanas were then moved to Venecia, a small dog-free island just off Santa Cruz. Other survivors were taken to the Darwin Station for captive breeding. This was the first attempt to breed land iguanas in captivity, and after initial setbacks, the program now shows much promise. With the elimination of feral dogs on Santa Cruz and Isabela, the captive-bred land iguanas have been repatriated, along with some of the iguanas that had been taken to Venecia. The next question is whether the iguana hatchlings will be able to withstand predation from feral cats.

Though also menaced by cats and dogs, marine iguanas are found throughout the archipelago in healthy numbers—estimated at between 200,000 to 300,000. Marine iguanas perished by the thousands during the 1982–83 El Niño, but high levels of reproduction have restored most of the loss in population.

As for the glorious birds of the Galápagos, the overall conservation picture is hazy because most species have never been surveyed. What we do know makes it clear, however, that they too have suffered from introduced animals. Special cases among the birds are the Galápagos Penguin and the Flightless Cormorant, which will continue to be especially vulnerable because of their restricted range and small numbers. An oil spill or a trauma such as human development of the coastline would threaten them seriously. Similarly, development of Galápagos lagoons would endanger the beautiful birds that live there, such as the flamingos, stilts, and ducks.

Of all Galápagos conservation stories, none has attracted wider attention and sympathy than that of the Dark-rumped Petrel. The petrels are commonly seen at sea within the Galápagos, and the population is substantial, perhaps 20,000 to 100,000. However, predation on their eggs and nestlings by rats, cats, dogs, and pigs has been so severe for the past few decades that scientists believe the petrel is doomed to extinction. Warding off the predators year after year will require a large investment of human time and energy. The only hopeful note is that many of the petrels may live in colonies that neither predators nor scientists have discovered.

One of the keys to saving the Galápagos fauna is regular monitoring. Vulnerable populations must be visited periodically to assess their numbers, distribution, and possible new threats. The naturalist guides

● *At the time of Darwin's visit in 1835, land iguanas were so abundant on Santiago and other islands that the* Beagle *crew had a hard time finding a "spot free from their burrows on which to pitch a single tent." A century and a half later, these stout-bodied, yellow-orange lizards thrive on only three relatively pristine islands.*

who accompany tour groups are important in this regard. Visiting the same locations over and over again, they become sensitive to changes in wildlife. Also important are scientists with special research permits for exploring areas of the islands that are seldom seen by human beings.

It seems eminently sensible to me to study fossils to piece together a picture showing where nature was heading before the great interruption caused by man. Guided by that picture, conservationists can make small adjustments or take bigger and bolder measures with some assurance that they are on the right track.

Today the most exciting conservation scenario for the Galápagos is the reintroduction of native species on islands where they lived before they felt the disruptive impact of man. Because the archipelago is relatively small, there are real possibilities for success, though there are also obvious limitations. Species that are totally extinct (not just extinct on a particular island) cannot be brought back, and on the four or five islands where man has had a continuous impact for a century or more, the original condition can never be regained.

But there are nearly pristine islands where repatriation could be successful and highly positive. For instance, the island of Rábida once supported native populations of tortoises and land iguanas which died out as a result of predators and increased competition for food sources. Ten years ago the last goats were removed, and the island, now entirely within the limits of the Galápagos National Park and with only one tourist trail, has no other introduced plants or animals. The lack of a dock means the introduction of black rats is unlikely—rats are poor swimmers and don't get off a boat unless it's tied to a dock—another reason why Rábida offers special promise as a repatriation site. Reintroducing tortoises and iguanas here would not only be a boon to these species but would also restore the island ecosystem to a more natural state by including the large herbivores that once lived there.

The point of this and other conservation efforts is not just nostalgia for an era of natural perfection that existed before man barged in and threw everything dangerously out of kilter. That time will never come again and pining for it is a waste of time and emotion. I think we must concentrate on what is rather than what was: the Galápagos remain comparatively unspoiled and we should apply our energies to keeping it that way.

Thus rather than continually castigating the human species, we should recognize that our potential swings between nobility and evil; in the Galápagos, there is ample evidence of both extremes. Rather than holding to a foolish hope that man will simply go away and leave the islands alone, we should recognize that man is now a permanent factor in the evolution of the Galápagos. And perhaps the Galápagos can be a factor in the spiritual evolution of man, teaching him the timeless virtue of its tame and humble heart as well as its striking lessons of evolution in progress.

In closing, a final salute to Darwin, whose writings are early witnesses to an engaged conservationist spirit. While subsequent research has refined many aspects of evolutionary theory and while modern techniques, unavailable in Darwin's time, have facilitated research, there is no doubt that his thinking still illuminates the terrain more than a century after his death. Writing about the *Beagle* expedition, Darwin lamented the "fate of most voyagers, no sooner to discover what is most interesting in any locality, than they are hurried from it." What he saw in those brief nineteen days ashore on the Galápagos, however, has become part of the foundation on which evolutionary science continues to build today. Our best way to honor him is to carry on the free pursuit of evolutionary knowledge, so that it too may evolve as new discoveries are made.

● *David Steadman feeds one of twenty adult tortoises housed at the Charles Darwin Research Station for breeding purposes.*

90

PART TWO

Introduction to the Plates

Even a fact-hunting, data-minded paleontologist has moments in the Galápagos when—perhaps watching the panorama of a blazing sunset over the Pacific—he remembers that nature is for the eye and the heart as well as for the mind.

In my trip to the islands in 1984 I added a less scientific, more aesthetic element in the form of my brother Lee, an artist whose color plates of Galápagos wildlife follow this introduction.

Lee's paintings are both art and science. They are art because of their aesthetic appeal and science because of their careful accuracy. Unlike renderings in some field guides, Lee's paintings attempt to go beyond mere depiction to give a sense of spontaneously meeting an animal up close in its natural habitat. They are watercolors and that seems appropriately informal; the Galápagos is a very informal place.

When Lee graduated from college in 1982 we began planning for him to join me on a Galápagos trip, both to paint the islands' residents and to assist me in the field. We left for a seven-week visit in July of 1984, returning in May 1985 for a second stay of three weeks.

This part of the book, presenting the resident wildlife of the Galápagos in a gallery of plates with accompanying descriptions, belongs as much to Lee as to me, so I thought he might tell some of his own story of painting on the islands.

● *Lee Steadman at home in Pennsylvania, 1986.*

Preceding page, a pioneering clump of brachycereus cactus gains a foothold in the barren surface of a young lava field.

During the year before we left for the Galápagos, I practiced by painting many of the islands' species, getting the feel of rendering them and also the feel of Dave constantly correcting inaccuracies. I had a fairly good idea of how the animals would look as Dave had shown me hundreds of color slides and I had worked with museum specimens and studied skins of birds from the Smithsonian's collections. Still there was no question that I had to see the wildlife in person if I intended to do it justice in a series of watercolors. Getting out in the field and seeing the real thing with your own eyes can give you a wealth of new ideas. You see poses flash by. You pick up things about movements, lighting, habitats, gestures, moods, personalities, moments of life—things you would never get from slides or skins.

My first impression of the islands was an unqualified jolt. I knew I wasn't heading for some latter-day Garden of Eden, but I was surprised anyway. I would have settled for just a little tropical enchantment, a few swaying palms and towering waterfalls, but what I got was an unrelieved vista of charred volcanic rock that reminded me of the Darwin quote that sounds like a description of hell—pitted lava, vapors rising from below, cones and craters everywhere. Every plant seems to be thorny; the surface is dry, rough, stark, harsh, very harsh. You go through places where you have to swing a machete for hours to cut through the brush, looking for a cave that might not even exist.

After a while, however, you start to realize that the islands are beautiful in their own special way as the impact of the pristine spots begins to grow on you. Images are so striking, so different—the wildlife, the climate, the expansive scapes. You might be tired and cut up from thorns and lava and then you realize you may have been the first human being on this spot for a hundred years or in all time. And you look around with new eyes— this is the Galápagos.

In our first seven weeks on the islands, Dave and I developed a fairly standard routine. In the morning we would do fossil research—in the caves or searching for new ones—and my job was mostly digging and carrying. Afternoons, Dave would start sifting and sorting the morning's haul while I took off to paint with a backpack filled with equipment. Since I had to carry everything myself, I quickly learned the advantage of sticking to essentials—a notebook, a block of watercolor paper, a palette, brushes, paint, pencils, a quart of water, a camera, and binoculars. The pack itself, when emptied, served as a welcome cushion against the hard, often jagged lava.

What struck me most as an artist was the blue of the tropical ocean— the bright, bright blue which I tried to capture in my marine iguana painting (plate 5). Inland, the Galápagos taught me lessons about color and light. I started out with a conventional range of colors but found myself refining my palette to catch the subtle, toned-down colors of the islands.

In the lowlands your first impression is almost that the islands were tossed in a washing machine and all the colors ran out—except for dull browns and greens and lots of black. Within this limited range, however, there is enormous richness and life. I think that learning to welcome this and work with it was a maturing step for me as an artist.

Another challenge was the weather. In the Galápagos it changes hour by hour and that means changes in light that have a distinct effect on the mood of a painting. Sometimes the sun is so bright that everything seems to glow with an incandescent light. A hour or two later, the garúa mist creeps in and landscapes become subdued and wet. (Unfortunately so does the artist—and his art supplies.)

I spent a lot of my time scouting for good backgrounds. Of the photos I took, 90 percent were not of animals but of scenes—rock formations, tidal pools, light playing on water. It is tempting to say my artistic fulfillment came primarily from choosing backgrounds. Natural selection determined how the animals looked but the rest was left to me.

Of course I didn't select backgrounds at random. The setting had to be correct, the habitat appropriate. Dave gave me lots of advice about where an animal would be and what it would be doing or eating. The chosen tree, shrub, herb, or beach had to be part of the informational as well as artistic composition of the painting. I tried to make the animal's involvement in the scene reflect reality. What I mean is, certain birds never dominate a landscape, no matter how narrow or confined that landscape might be. A Black Rail, for instance, is inconspicuous slinking through tall grasses and sedges in a highland setting. Add the normal shroud of highland fog and the bird is hardly the star of the painting, but the overall scene gives the right proportion.

A question people often ask about wildlife painting is: How do you get the animals to stand still? Of course they realize animals don't pose like a model in the studio, but how does the artist manage to fix them in an image? Audubon's technique was the shotgun. Since he shot most of the

● *An eroded pinnacle of volcanic tuff presides over the rocky coast of Santiago.*

95

birds he painted himself, the specimens he worked with were fresh. He could take each feather and stretch it out and the colors remained true—even of the eyes, beak, and feet—as long as he worked fast.

In the Galápagos conservation regulations forbid shooting animals. Of course we wouldn't want to shoot them anyway, but on the islands the wild-life is so tame that it is not even necessary. The animals don't exactly stand still, but they're unfrightened and allow you to approach, almost as if you were one of them. In Pennsylvania I've spent as many as eight hours cam-ouflaged and sitting up in a tree in complete silence, waiting to get a quick glimpse of a deer. In the islands, the animals often simply ignore you—other times they seem to go out of their way to attract your attention. The Galápagos may well be the best place in the world to make wildlife sketches.

Once I was concentrating on painting a dove and I reached back to my palette and found a mockingbird walking through my paint. (If it had been a booby, I might have been tempted to think this was the explanation for the famous blue feet.) Another time I was on the beach painting a flamingo when a sea lion charged up behind me. I must have been totally absorbed in the bird because I didn't even hear the sea lion coming, and a sea lion on land is scarcely a master of stealth. Despite all I've said about the tameness of species, it scared the wits out of me to find myself in what was obviously this sea lion's favorite spot. The unfinished sketch would have to wait—I backed off.

The last thing you want to do when painting in the field is to make a place react to you—you should react to it instead. We were raised this way in Pennsylvania when it came to going into the woods. Be a passive pres-ence, not an invader bashing through. Make no noise, leave no tracks. If you eat an orange, pick up the peels. If you took it in, you take it out.

My favorite painting, reproduced here as plate 13, is of the Dark-rumped Petrel. The bird's wings are fully extended as it cruises, a potent power, in full flight between the waves. Normally you would only get a glance at one of these birds, even with high-power binoculars, but some local people found an injured petrel on the beach which I could study. I doubt if any other artist has been able to work from a real, living, up-close sample, so my painting may be one of the most accurate depictions of this bird. I spent months turning this dramatic image around in my mind before I fin-ished the painting.

A finished work begins with a field sketch. You find a good spot, put the pad on your lap, and go to work. A sketch usually takes a few hours. What you concentrate on in the field is the observation aspect; quick sketch-ing is the equivalent of note-taking. Sometimes I would add touch-ups or accents that evening back at camp, to make the sketch more exciting, but the real artistic polishing comes later.

In fact it might come months later, when you are back home in your own studio. You start thinking about the final painting, making thumb-nail sketches to work out the pose and composition and background. You do

• A hardened lava flow now forms the gentle curve of a tidal inlet on Fer-nandina.

Opposite, Greater Flamingo—
See plate 35.

96

some detailed sketches—for instance, the feather structure on a wing.

Then you start adding up everything you have gleaned from museum skins and slides and your own photography and visual memory. And your brother. You make more sketches, work on poses, add detail, and mull over new ideas. For instance, with Dave's advice I decided to group different species of Darwin's finches in four plates so they could be easily compared. For the reptiles and rodents, I painted only a representative sample of the Galápagos varieties. Painting each of many races would have been redundant artistically and not significant informationally because the anatomical differences are so minor that it takes an expert to appreciate them. We deliberately departed from the normal practice of showing only adult males of a species to include females and "immatures."

Getting a drawing that is artistically and scientifically on the mark can be a struggle, maybe two weeks of work. But then you are ready to forge ahead and make the final painting. This part of the process can go amazingly fast, sometimes taking only a day or two. But since watercolor is such an unforgiving medium, it takes weeks to get to the point where you can get it right in one finished painting.

A lot of people don't realize that the best images of wildlife are painted, not photographed. In field guides and even for scientific illustration, the artist can catch subtleties that photography often misses. A painting can do better justice to the nuances of highlighting and lighting. The diagnostic points emerge clearly since you can edit out the extraneous material that often detracts in a photograph. I think wildlife painting adds texture and depth of character, the way an oil painting tends to be better than a good photographic portrait.

Of course wildlife art is very popular now. I'm not sure why, maybe because we're so urbanized and suburbanized that people miss nature. Perhaps a painting on the wall helps us remember what it was like before parks and protected enclaves became, for many, the only taste of "the wild." I only hope that artists who specialize in nature art try to paint or draw with feeling—not only for the animal or landscape but also for the work itself, as an artistic statement rather than a mere picture. Aesthetic values like composition, color, mood, and depth make all the difference if the viewer is to take away a sense of value.

From painting nature in the Galápagos I've come back to painting nature in Pennsylvania. I have a fledgling idea for a series of giant watercolors, 6 feet by 3 or 4 feet. The paintings are done in the woods and will include human figures, almost life-sized. The humans are passive, just visitors passing through. They come and go—the forest stays.

PLATES

A Note on the Inclusion of Species

The following color plates are the only illustrations I know
of in which representatives of all native vertebrates of the
Galápagos are depicted in color and with scientific accuracy.
Every resident species of bird is included as well as at least
one species of each major group of reptiles and mammals.
A few extinct species, important to my work on the islands,
are also depicted.

The caption facing each plate provides information
about the evolution of the species, much of which I have
developed from my own research. The focus on evolution is
supplemented by descriptions of the unusual behavior of
some of the Galápagos animals, drawn from personal experience and observation. The distribution of reptile and
mammal species is presented in an appendix following the
plates. Since the more complex distribution of birds is difficult to summarize, a discussion of range is included in the
plate captions for bird species. For a detailed review of the
biology of each species, the reader may consult the scientific
literature listed in the bibliography.

D.W.S.

PLATE 1

Galápagos Tortoise *Geochelone elephantopus*

Tortoises have played a major role in the natural and human history of the Galápagos. In fact the Spanish word *galápagos* means tortoises and was given to the islands because of the wonderful abundance of tortoises that early explorers found there.

The Galápagos tortoise consists of a single species that was, until recently, found on all major islands except Genovesa, Marchena, Culpepper, and Wenman. The most characteristic feature of the tortoise is its shell, which consists of an upper half (the carapace) and a lower half (the plastron). "Domed-shell," "saddle-backed," and "intermediate" are three basic types of carapaces in Galápagos tortoises. The domed-shell tortoises tend to be larger overall with relatively short legs and necks. In saddle-backed tortoises, such as "Onan the Magnificent," the aged but spirited tortoise from Pinzón depicted here, the front of the carapace is raised along the midline, thus allowing greater elevation of the elongated neck. Variations occur within each shell type, including the populations regarded as intermediate, although each adult population can be categorized as being one type or another.

An interesting situation occurs on the largest island of Isabela, where five of the six major volcanoes are inhabited by distinctive subspecies of tortoises. These populations are isolated from each other by stretches of extremely arid, inhospitable terrain that includes much treacherous "aa" lava. Nobody knows whether the tortoises colonized Isabela when the island was divided into six separate islands (each consisting of one of the major volcanoes) or whether the colonization occurred after further volcanic activity had merged the smaller islands into the one huge island now known as Isabela. Nevertheless, the barren lavas that separate the different volcanoes are just as effective a barrier to tortoises as the ocean that once separated the volcanoes.

The tortoises on San Cristóbal are the most distinctive in the islands and those from Española are the next most distinctive. This trend occurs in other species of reptiles, mammals, and birds in the Galápagos, where the east-to-west flow of currents and winds means that east-to-west colonization is the rule. Because it is unlikely that San Cristóbal and Española would have been colonized by tortoises from the central or western islands, the tortoises on these two islands probably have been isolated longer than others. With its extreme eastern location and large size, San Cristóbal probably was the island where tortoises first colonized the Galápagos.

The Galápagos tortoise differs in many respects from any of the three species of tortoises still living in mainland South America. This suggests that the Galápagos tortoise may have evolved from an extinct species of mainland tortoise. During the Pleistocene ice ages and before, various forms of large tortoises lived in North America, South America, the West Indies, Africa, and Asia. It is among these extinct continental forms that we should search for the nearest relative of the Galápagos tortoise.

PLATE 2

Green Turtle *Chelonia mydas*

Yellow-bellied Sea Snake *Pelamis platurus*

The green turtle, or green sea turtle, is found throughout warm waters of the Atlantic, Pacific, and Indian oceans. Between 1,200 and 3,500 female green turtles nest each year in the Galápagos, where there are seven main nesting beaches on six different islands. Green turtles also concentrate in several feeding grounds within the archipelago, some of which are not near the main nesting beaches. Other kinds of marine turtles recorded from Galápagos waters are the hawksbill (*Eretmochelys imbricata*), olive ridley (*Lepidochelys olivacea*), and leatherback (*Dermochelys coriacea*), although none of these species has been known to nest in the islands.

The Galápagos form of green turtle is found in much of the eastern Pacific. Typically it has a browner (less green) and more steeply domed carapace than most other subspecies. Galápagos green turtles occur in two color phases, the brown phase and the less common yellow phase. These two color phases do not seem to be correlated with differences in age or sex, although the "yellow" green turtles may be nonbreeders that inhabit the Galápagos only seasonally.

During the 1970s, Derek Green of the University of Texas, a specialist in the study of sea turtles, tagged nearly 6,000 green turtles, mostly nesting females, within the Galápagos. Twenty-three of the tagged turtles were recovered along the Pacific coast of Costa Rica, Panama, Colombia,

Ecuador, and Peru. Three of the recoveries were of males, which is very significant since much less is known about the long-distance movements of males than females. One female turtle recovered along the coast of Ecuador had nested previously in the Galápagos, and she subsequently returned to the Galápagos to nest again. This suggests that green turtles from the Galápagos may interbreed with their coastal relatives, which would explain why they have not developed any characteristics distinct from green turtles found elsewhere in the eastern Pacific.

The yellow-bellied sea snake is a venomous, highly pelagic species that ranges nearly throughout the tropical Pacific Ocean, from the Indonesian region east to the American coast from Ecuador to Mexico. Although this species probably does not have a resident population in the Galápagos, we have included it here so that visitors to the islands may become more aware of this beautiful animal.

The yellow-bellied sea snake is a regular visitor to the Galápagos, but it is not known to breed in the cold waters of the archipelago. Sea snakes found in the Galápagos probably come from the breeding areas in the Gulf of Guayaquil (Ecuador) and the Gulf of Panama, where the ocean is much warmer.

PLATE 3

Leaf-toed Gecko   *Phyllodactylus* sp.

Lava Lizard   *Tropidurus* sp.

Galápagos lizards belong to two very different families, the Gekkonidae (geckos) and the Iguanidae (iguanas and lava lizards). Geckos are found throughout warm areas of the world. Most geckos are nocturnal and insectivorous. Scales on the bottom of their broad, flat toes function as suction cups that allow most geckos to walk up and down vertical surfaces, or even upside down on ceilings or horizontal branches.

The native geckos of the Galápagos are "leaf-toed" geckos. These tiny lizards are not readily seen by the casual observer. In fact, unless you turn over rocks or fallen tree trunks, or peel the bark from dead or dying trees and cacti, you could spend years in the Galápagos and never be aware of the presence of leaf-toed geckos, although they are abundant. Lee has depicted one here in the shadow of a rock.

That leaf-toed geckos should have colonized the islands is not at all surprising. These geckos are well represented along the arid Pacific coast of South America, from Ecuador to Chile. In northwestern Peru, for example, four different species of leaf-toed geckos may be found in the same coastal area, with habits not very different from their Galápagos relatives.

Some scholars suggest that two separate colonizations of leaf-toed geckos occurred during Galápagos history, and that the descendants of one of these invasions constitute the Wenman species, whereas geckos from the second invasion evolved into all other native populations. I believe that it is just as likely that leaf-toed geckos colonized the Galápagos only once. With time, the populations on each island developed differences in coloration, overall size, the size of various body parts, and the pattern and number of scales, especially the enlarged scales on the head and back.

Lava lizards are small but far more conspicuous than the geckos, since they are active by day, perched on rocks, searching for insects and other small invertebrates. Depicted here are a female (top) and male (middle). It is easy to identify lava lizards since they are shaped rather like a small iguana, long and slim, while geckos are much stockier and have conspicuously fat toes. Lava lizards live on all major islands, including those where tortoises and even geckos may be absent. The largest lava lizards are from Española. Those on Floreana are so subject to predation by the island's abundant cats and black rats that they seldom live long enough to reach full size; I would frankly predict their total extinction on Floreana within a few years. Like leaf-toed geckos, only a single species of lava lizard inhabits any particular island, but I believe they too colonized the Galápagos only once.

PLATE 4

Land Iguana *Conolophus subcristatus*

The land iguana is a large, herbivorous lizard. When not feeding, sunning, or engaging in reproductive or territorial activities, these lizards occupy burrows that they excavate in loose soil. Healthy populations of land iguanas exist today only on Santa Fé and Fernandina. Predation by dogs, cats, rats, and humans has wiped out the land iguanas on Santa Cruz, Baltra, and Santiago, and reduced their numbers on Isabela. On Rábida, they are known only from fossils.

The population of land iguanas from Santa Fé is often regarded as a distinct species. It differs from other land iguanas by being a paler, grayer shade of yellow and having a more distinct row of scaly spines along the back. The land iguanas from Isabela and Fernandina may also be distinct from the others.

The origins of both the land and the marine iguanas are evolutionary mysteries. Both are endemic to the Galápagos, and their relationships with other iguanas are uncertain. Several other large species of iguanas live in mainland Central America, South America, and the West Indies, with aberrant species found in Fiji, Tonga, and Madagascar. Yet based on the anatomy of bones and muscles, Galápagos land iguanas are more similar to Galápagos marine iguanas than to any of the iguanas outside of the islands. This would seem to suggest a common ancestry for the land iguana and marine iguana from a single colonization from the mainland, but recent biochemical studies point rather to separate colonizations by different mainland species.

The fossil record has not produced any evidence of the origins of either land iguanas or marine iguanas. Yet I believe that the nearest relatives of each of these iguanas may have lived in South America until only about 10,000 years ago. We know from fossil studies that many now extinct species of vertebrates lived along the Pacific coast of Ecuador and Peru until the end of the last Pleistocene ice age. Although the fossil record for reptiles is poorly known in this region, it is feasible that one or more species of large iguanas disappeared at this time of rapidly changing climates and habitats. Hunting and habitat alteration by humans may have been another cause of the extinction of iguanas along the Pacific coast of South America. Archaeologists have discovered evidence of large human populations in coastal Ecuador and Peru during prehistoric times. The past century has shown us how rapidly iguanas in the Galápagos and the West Indies can be decimated by human predation, since in Central and South America, native people even today consider iguana meat a delicacy.

It is interesting that the fossil skull of an iguana discovered on the island of Barbuda in the West Indies is very similar to the skull of the Galápagos land iguana. Unfortunately, this single fragmentary specimen cannot be identified positively enough to justify any valid specualtion about relationships between West Indian iguanas and the Galápagos land iguana.

PLATE 5

Marine Iguana *Amblyrhynchus cristatus*

The marine iguana is second only to the tortoise in terms of herpetological interest in the Galápagos. Marine iguanas are found nearly throughout the archipelago in coastal concentrations of up to 4,500 individuals per mile. The total population has been estimated at between 200,000 and 300,000. Although all marine iguanas are regarded as a single species, they vary in size and color from island to island. The marine iguanas from Santa Cruz, Isabela, and Fernandina are the largest; those from Española and Genovesa are the smallest. The marine iguanas from Española are brightly colored in shades of red, whereas those from Genovesa are uniformly flat black or dark gray. Lee painted these iguanas on Santa Cruz, where, as on Isabela and Fernandina, the adult male marine iguanas are beautifully blotched in shades of gray, black, green, and red. All juvenile marine iguanas are black.

The marine iguana feeds on marine algae, both underwater and in the intertidal zone, where it grazes above the water line on algae exposed by low tides. Marine iguanas also eat crustaceans, grasshoppers, and sea lion afterbirth on occasion. From this evidence we might speculate on the evolution of feeding habits of marine iguanas, beginning with an iguana that was a beach (littoral) and intertidal scavenger, then gradually became more marine and more herbivorous in its appetite. Feeding on seashore crustaceans has been recorded in lizards from the Philippines, Cerralvo

Island in the Gulf of California, Malpelo Island off Columbia, and on Nossi Be Island near Madagascar. There is little doubt that the marine iguana is the most marine-adapted species of lizard alive today, with a short, blunt snout for grazing on algae and a laterally compressed tail for swimming propulsion. Nevertheless, when compared with other lizards of the seashore, we see that the marine iguana is not in a class by itself.

If iguanas were among the first colonists of the Galápagos, they may have been land animals that turned to the sea for food because of the scarcity of terrestrial food resources. The early progenitors of the marine iguana might have searched the intertidal zone for food and turned to feeding on algae as well as crustaceans. On the other hand, if marine iguanas evolved from a marine species that became extinct on the mainland only relatively recently (see discussion of land iguanas), many or all of its marine adaptations may have been developed already on the mainland. Indeed, I would not be greatly surprised if bones of the marine iguana were discovered some day in an archaeological midden or Pleistocene fossil site along the coast of Ecuador or Peru. Certainly, such a discovery would clarify once and for all whether the marine iguana and land iguana evolved from a common ancestor or colonized the Galápagos independently.

PLATE 6

Galápagos Snakes   *Alsophis* sp.

The three species of terrestrial snakes are the most poorly studied group of reptiles in the Galápagos. Two of the species are widespread in the central and western islands. The third species is confined to San Cristóbal, Española, Floreana, and some of their small satellite islands. This pattern of distribution is very similar to that of all other terrestrial reptiles in the Galápagos; namely, the southeastern islands are inhabited by more distinctive forms than the central and western islands.

Unlike other types of reptiles in the Galápagos, which invariably have one species per island, there are two species of snakes on Santa Cruz, Baltra, Rábida, Santiago, Isabela, and Fernandina. This demonstrates multiple colonizations of single islands. Galápagos rice rats and Darwin's finches are the only other groups of Galápagos vertebrates in which more than one species colonized the same island. As with the rice rats, no more than two species of snakes are found on any particular island.

Galápagos snakes are either striped or spotted, although both striped and spotted individuals are found in certain populations of both species. Characters that help to define the species will not be readily evident to the casual observer. They include the presence or absence of pits on certain scales of the back, side, or tail; the number of scales on the belly; the scale pattern of the head and neck; and the number of rows of scales on the back and sides. Striped or spotted snakes may fall into several of the possible combinations of these categories.

It seems likely that a single colonization from the mainland produced the entire radiation of Galápagos snakes. They are similar to a species of snake with scale-pits (*Alsophis chamissonis*, no common name available) that lives in coastal Chile and Peru. Certainly the range of *Alsophis chamissonis* makes it eligible for colonization of the Galápagos and there are clear anatomical similarities between *Alsophis chamissonis* (and two other Peruvian species) and the Galápagos snakes.

The future of snakes on the inhabited islands of the Galápagos is not promising. Unfortunately, we cannot plan effectively to save these beautiful animals unless we can learn something about their habits. The sad truth is that few animals are more difficult to study than snakes.

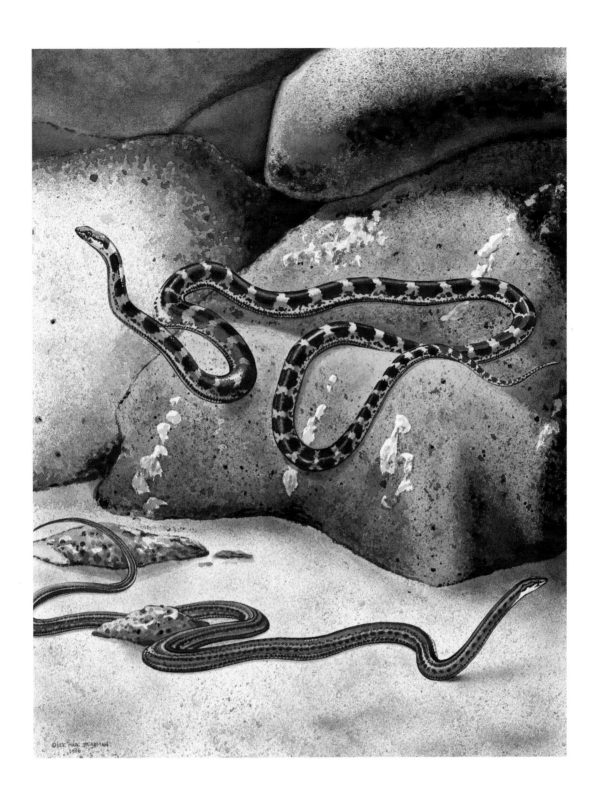

PLATE 7

Red Bat   *Lasiurus borealis*

Hoary Bat   *Lasiurus cinereus*

Bats are represented in the Galápagos by two species, the red bat (top) and the hoary bat (bottom). The red bat has been recorded alive only from San Cristóbal and Santa Cruz, but I have also found its fossils on Floreana. The hoary bat lives only on Santa Cruz, and I have found no fossil remains at all of this bat. Bats have been seen flying on Isabela but so far none has been identified. The small bats seen commonly at night on Santa Cruz, especially near the Charles Darwin Research Station, are probably red bats. Unfortunately, not much else is known about Galápagos bats. Since both species roost singly or in small groups in thick vegetation, they are difficult to observe.

Both the red bat and hoary bat are widespread on the American continents, being found in a variety of habitats from northern North America to southern South America. The northern populations are migratory, and some tropical populations may be migratory as well, so these two species are likely candidates for bat colonization of oceanic islands. Both species have been recorded in winter on Bermuda, which is about as far offshore in the Atlantic (600 miles) as the Galápagos Islands are from the Pacific coast of South America, and the hoary bat has even colonized the Hawaiian Islands, which are more than 2,000 miles from North America.

I believe that the red bat colonized the Galápagos earlier than the hoary bat, since the Galápagos variety of red bat differs anatomically from those of the mainland, whereas hoary bats are identical with mainland populations. Also, I have found fossils of the red bat in deposits that are several thousand years old, but no remains of the hoary bat have yet been found in any of the Galápagos fossil sites. Furthermore, the hoary bat was not recorded from the Galápagos until two specimens were taken on Santa Cruz in 1952, and all subsequent specimens have also been obtained from this island. All this strongly suggests that the hoary bat colonized Santa Cruz only very recently, and has dispersed little or not at all to the other islands.

PLATE 8

Galápagos Fur Seal   *Arctocephalus galapagoensis*

Seals, sea lions, and walruses constitute an order of marine mammals known as the "pinnipeds." The Galápagos Islands are the only place where pinnipeds live on the equator. The two resident pinnipeds are this Galápagos fur seal and the California sea lion depicted in the next plate. The unexpected existence of these species on the equator depends on the upwellings of cool nutrient-rich water where plankton and fish are abundant.

There are several important differences between fur seals and sea lions. The Galápagos fur seal is smaller than the California sea lion. The average weights of males and females are, respectively, 140 and 60 lbs. for the fur seal, and 440 and 180 lbs. for the sea lion. The fur seal has very thick, luxuriant fur, whereas the sea lion is sparsely furred. The most obvious ecological difference between the Galápagos fur seal and the sea lion in the Galápagos is their choice of onshore habitat. Sea lions live in large colonies on beaches or other areas of protected waters, whereas fur seals live in much smaller, more scattered groups along steep, rocky seashores. Both species are found nearly throughout the Galápagos wherever suitable habitat exists, although the largest numbers of fur seals occur on Isabela, Fernandina, Marchena, and Pinta, all islands with a maximal upwelling of cool water.

Fur seals and sea lions also differ significantly in terms of how they obtain food, which consists mainly of fish and squid. Within the Galápagos, for example, fur seals feed mostly at night and at shallow depths (average depth of 85 feet, with a maximum depth of 280 feet), whereas sea lions do their fishing mostly during the day, diving to greater depths (average depth of 130 feet, with a maximum depth of 600 feet).

The Galápagos fur seal is an endemic species that has evolved from the closely related South American fur seal (*Arctocephalus australis*), which is found today from southernmost Chile and Argentina north to southern Brazil in the Atlantic and to central Peru in the Pacific. The South American fur seal weighs, on the average, about twice as much as the Galápagos fur seal. Otherwise, the two species are very similar in appearance. Colonization of the Galápagos probably occurred during a glacial interval or "ice age," when cool waters extended farther north along the Pacific coast of South America, allowing the range of the South American fur seal to expand northward.

The fur seal depicted here is an adult female that visited Lee and me at Punta Pitt on San Cristóbal. After a long day of exploring for fossil localities, we went to the rocky shoreline in the late afternoon with our handlines to catch some fish. No catch would mean another evening of rice and beans. The fur seal swam around right where we wanted to fish, preventing us from throwing our lines into the water. After a while, however, she came ashore and flopped up to within 3 feet of us. She remained here for quite a while, providing our best observation of a fur seal. And while she was ashore we grabbed the chance to catch our supper.

PLATE 9

California Sea Lion *Zalophus californianus*

The sea lion that lives in the Galápagos is an endemic subspecies of the California sea lion, a species well known as the "trained seal" of circuses. The playful nature of this species, especially the young pups, is apparent to anyone who has done much swimming in the Galápagos. However, the aggressive nature of adult males, or females with young, becomes equally apparent to those who get too close.

Other populations of the California sea lion are found in the Sea of Japan and along the Pacific coast of North America from Vancouver to Sinaloa, Mexico. As with fur seals, the sea lions of the Galápagos are smaller than their nearest relatives on the continent. Compared with those from California and Mexico, male sea lions in the Galápagos average about 100 lbs. lighter, and females 50 lbs. lighter. Because these differences are not as great as those that distinguish the Galápagos fur seal from its founding species, the sea lions in the Galápagos are generally classified, rather arbitrarily, as an endemic subspecies rather than as an endemic species.

Whereas the fur seal colonized the Galápagos from South America, the sea lion must have colonized the Galápagos from the north. This would be difficult to explain in light of today's oceanographic conditions, specifically, the warm waters and ocean currents that the sea lions would have to buck to reach this far south. During the glacial intervals of the past two million years, however, cooler waters extended farther south along the Pacific coasts of North and Central America, punctuated by the return of warmer waters as the glaciers retreated. Sea lions probably colonized the Galápagos during such a period, and then were cut off from their northern range by the return of relatively warm and fishless waters.

© LEE MARK STEADMAN
1987

PLATE 10

Santa Fé Rice Rat *Oryzomys bauri*

Large Santa Cruz Rice Rat *Nesoryzomys indefessus*

Small Santa Cruz Rice Rat *Nesoryzomys darwini*

Santa Cruz Giant Rat *Megaoryzomys curioi*

Native rodents once dominated the mammal fauna of the Galápagos, although only three species survive today. The Galápagos rodents consist of three main groups: true rice rats (genus *Oryzomys*); Galápagos rice rats (genus *Nesoryzomys*); and Galápagos giant rats (*Megaoryzomys*). Each of these groups represents a separate colonization of cricetine (mouselike) rodents from mainland South America.

A continental species of true rice rat, (*Oryzomys xantheolus*), is very similar to the true rice rat found on San Cristóbal and Santa Fé in the Galápagos. Rather than being a historic, human-assisted introduction from the mainland, as others have suggested, I believe that the San Cristóbal and Santa Fé rice rats evolved from *Oryzomys xantheolus*, which reached the islands on floating masses of debris washed off the mainland and carried westward by ocean currents, perhaps as recently as several thousand years ago.

Charles Darwin captured living specimens of the San Cristóbal rice rat in 1835, yet within the next couple of decades rice rats became extinct on San Cristóbal. In 1984, Godfrey Merlen, brother Lee, and I found thousands of fossils of this rice rat in several sites on San Cristóbal, the only specimens collected since Darwin's time. When we get radiocarbon dates on these rice rat fossils, we will have a better idea of how long before Darwin's time these rodents were present on the island.

The Santa Fé rice rat (right center) is very similar to the San Cristóbal rice rat and doubtless evolved from animals that colonized from San Cristóbal. The Santa Fé rice rat still thrives today and is the only native rodent in the Galápagos whose behavior and ecology have been extensively studied. Like most rodents, Santa Fé rice rats are active mainly after dark. They eat a variety of plants, especially grass seeds, and small invertebrates, and they breed during the rainy season when food is abundant. In turn, the rice rats are eaten by hawks, owls, and snakes. Galápagos rice rats are the second major group of native rodents. Their continental origin is a mystery. The first of the two subgroups of Galápagos rice rats consists of five large species, one each on Santiago, Rábida, Isabela, and Fernandina, and another on both Santa Cruz (depicted here, upper left) and Baltra. The second subgroup consists of three small species, one each on Santa Cruz (left center), Isabela, and Fernandina. The large species from Rábida and Isabela and the small species from Isabela are known only from fossils. The small species from Fernandina was first discovered from fresh owl pellets collected in 1979. Because the only surviving species of Galápagos rice rats are those from Fernandina, there is very little chance that any future natural dispersal will occur.

The third major group of native rodents in the Galápagos consists of the extinct giant rats. The larger of the two species is known only from fossil deposits on Santa Cruz. In 1984, our field party collected numerous fossils on Isabela of smaller species of giant rat, which had previously been known from only a few, fragmentary remains. It is interesting and somewhat puzzling that the closest mainland relatives of the giant rat are rodents of the genus *Thomasomys* that live today mainly in Andean forests above 3,000 feet elevation. But characters of the skull and teeth clearly show that giant rats of the Galápagos have evolved from *Thomasomys* rather than from any of the mainland rice rats. In painting the giant rat depicted here in the foreground, Lee has given it a furry coat typical of mainland species of *Thomasomys* on the assumption that it would have closely resembled the mainland forms.

Aside from their scientific interest, the rice rats that live on Santa Fé and Fernandina are a source of amusement and frustration for those who explore these islands. Mammalogist David Clark noted that he was forced to keep his tent open on Santa Fé, for otherwise the rice rats would chew through the tent in order to inspect the contents. My own experiences with the Santa Fé rice rat have been similar; their nocturnal curiosity is insatiable.

PLATE II

Galápagos Penguin   *Spheniscus mendiculus*

That a penguin should live on the equator might seem strange at first, for we normally associate penguins with the frigid Antarctic region. Indeed, it would be most unusual to find penguins living in Trinidad, Zanzibar, or New Guinea, yet the endemic Galápagos Penguin actually is not out of place on the equatorial shores of Isabela and Fernandina. Like the Flightless Cormorant, the Galápagos Penguin lives where the upwelling of cool, nutrient-rich waters results in abundant food in the form of small fish. The nesting of the Galápagos Penguin is intimately related to yearly fluctuations in local weather conditions, with high rates of nesting success during cool, dry years and low rates of nesting success during warm, wet years. The 1982–83 El Niño was an especially bad time for Galápagos Penguins.

The Galápagos Penguin was first described formally in 1871, based on a specimen collected in 1852 by Dr. Kinberg of the Swedish frigate *Eugenie*. Andrew Bloxam, a naturalist aboard the British ship *Blonde* that stopped in the Galápagos for two days in 1824 or 1825 en route to the Hawaiian Islands, was the first to report seeing penguins, but Bloxam was not impressed to find them living in the islands. As he wrote in a letter to William Swainson (quoted in Walter Rothschild's *Avifauna of Laysan*), "I met only with one species of the penguins there, which was small and nothing remarkable about it."

The Galápagos Penguin is very closely related to the Peruvian Penguin (*Spheniscus humboldti*), which is found all along the Pacific Coast of South America from central Chile through most of Peru. In fact, the Peruvian Penguin and the Galápagos Penguin are so similar that the latter must have evolved directly from the former. The Peruvian Penguin has been found to nest as far north in Peru as 6° south latitude, and even wanders north into Ecuador to only 1° south of the equator, the identical latitude inhabited by the Galápagos Penguin. Thus the Galápagos Penguin, so often mentioned as the world's only equatorial penguin, actually shares this honor with its mainland relative.

My most memorable encounter with the Galápagos Penguin was in 1978 at Post Office Bay on Floreana, where four of us were waiting at the shore for a boat back to Santa Cruz. We entertained ourselves by looking at birds, particularly the Blue-footed Boobies that were dive-bombing fish in the shallow bay. Four Galápagos Penguins appeared about 100 yards offshore, paddling around in the calm water. They slowly swam closer until one of the penguins swam all the way to shore, jumped out of the water, and waddled right up to us. From only a foot away, and at the level of my knees, this bold bird cocked its head and looked up at us, posing graciously as I shot two entire rolls of film.

PLATE 12

Waved Albatross   *Diomedea leptorhyncha*

The Waved Albatross, also known as the Galápagos Albatross, nests only on Isla Española in the Galápagos and on Isla La Plata, just off the coast of Ecuador. The colony on Isla La Plata is very small, so the survival of the species depends mainly on the much larger colony of about 12,000 pairs on Española.

No living species of albatross seems to be closely related to the Waved Albatross. This relatively large, stocky species of albatross is in a size-class that was widespread until sometime during the Pleistocene ice ages. Almost certainly the species of albatross that gave rise to the Waved Albatross is extinct. Fossils, especially from the eastern Pacific region, might shed light on the evolution of the Waved Albatross. Thus far I have found no albatross fossils in the Galápagos.

Unlike most species of albatross, the Waved Albatross is not a great wanderer at sea. It has been recorded outside of the Galápagos only in the equatorial eastern Pacific, especially off the coasts of Ecuador and Peru.

The history of the scientific naming of the Waved Albatross is unusual. It was originally named *Diomedea leptorhyncha* by the famous ornithologist Elliott Coues in 1866, based on a skull received at the Smithsonian Institution from an unknown donor and without reference to the locality where it was found. Coues noted differences between this skull and those of several other species of albatross. In 1883 Osbert Salvin, of the British Museum (Natural History), studied the skin of an albatross collected along the Peruvian coast, which he assumed to be a new species and named *Diomedea irrorata*. Since he was not familiar with the skull in the Smithsonian, Salvin did not realize that the species he was describing (which later became known commonly as the Waved Albatross) was in fact the same species already named by Coues. A century later, in 1971, George Watson (then of the Smithsonian) and George Divoky reexamined the skull described by Coues and determined it was the same as Salvin's Waved Albatross. Coues's long-ignored name actually has priority over Salvin's, and the Waved Albatross may thus be known as *Diomedea leptorhyncha* rather than *Diomedea irrorata*.

The story offers a good illustration of the importance of maintaining long-term collections in museums. If Coues's 1866 specimen had not been safely and properly maintained for more than a century in the Division of Birds at the Smithsonian, its history would have remained confused. As decades become centuries, museums like the Smithsonian allow researcher after researcher, from all over the world, to examine and reexamine specimens. This free pursuit of knowledge is essential, for as ideas and technologies change, we can look at old specimens in new ways that lead us to reinterpret their meaning.

PLATE 13

Dark-rumped Petrel   *Pterodroma phaeopygia*

The Dark-rumped Petrel, also known as the Hawaiian Petrel, is the only true petrel that resides in the Galápagos. A smaller edition of the Dark-rumped Petrel lives in the Hawaiian Islands. The Dark-rumped Petrel has been recorded along the eastern Pacific coast from Mexico to Peru, yet it is not known to nest on any of the coastal islands. I would not be surprised, however, if the prehistoric breeding range of this species included coastal islands. Based on the extreme vulnerability of the Dark-rumped Petrel to introduced mammals, it might be that populations of Dark-rumped Petrels in the eastern Pacific became extinct and disappeared before they could be recorded by scientific collectors.

Seen at sea nearly anywhere in the archipelago, Dark-rumped Petrels nest in the moist highlands of San Cristóbal, Floreana, Santa Cruz, Isabela, and Santiago. Like many other species of petrels, they nest in burrows they excavate in soft soil. Fossils from the arid lowlands of Floreana show that Dark-rumped Petrels have not always been restricted to the moist highlands, and that these nesting areas actually represent their last retreat from the predation of introduced mammals.

The following passage, from the field notes of the 1906 California Academy of Sciences Expedition, gives an excellent picture of petrel behavior in the populous colonies of that time:

During the breeding season they were active over the land at night. A party from the Academy in camp near the summit of James Island [Santiago] on August 7 were kept awake by their incessant call-notes, uttered as the birds flew about just above the tree tops. At Indefatigable Island [Santa Cruz] they congregated close inshore at dusk and circled over the water in loose flocks, from which individuals were constantly ascending in great spirals to the height of several hundred feet, when they headed inland. In the interior of the island they were particularly prominent during two hours after sunset and during two hours before sunrise, there being an evening flight to the land and a morning flight away from it. While members of the Expedition were in the forest belt of Indefatigable Island in November, these petrels were frequently seen and heard in the nighttime as they flew overhead, but in January none were met with on the island, the land apparently having been forsaken for the sea.

As is true for many species of petrels, the nearest relatives of the Dark-rumped Petrel have not been determined, although the Black-capped Petrel of the West Indies (*Pterodroma hasitata*) and the Juan Fernandez Petrel of the South Pacific (*Pterodroma externa*) are similar in plumage. Perhaps the nearest relative of the Dark-rumped Petrel is a species whose only remains are bones lying in Polynesian archaeological sites. Innumerable populations of petrels, and an unknown number of entire species, have been lost in the Pacific because of human activity during the past few thousand years.

PLATE 14

Audubon's Shearwater   *Puffinus lherminieri*

The other resident member of the procellariid family (fulmars, shearwaters, petrels, and prions) in the Galápagos is Audubon's Shearwater, also known as the Dusky Shearwater, Dusky-backed Shearwater, or Galápagos Shearwater. Audubon's Shearwater is found in tropical seas around the world. It is most often seen within sight of land and is particularly common near cliffs along the coast, where it nests either in crevices or, like the petrels, in burrows in soft soil. The fluttery flight of this species, on shallow wingbeats just above the water, is a familiar sight to mariners.

Audubon's Shearwaters are common and widespread in the islands, although their exact nesting distribution is poorly known. The Galápagos population is an endemic race distinguished by small overall size, dark upperparts, lack of dark breast patches, considerable white on the underparts, heavily patterned flank feathers, and a short tail. Galápagos birds have been recorded off the coasts of Panama, Colombia, and Ecuador, and rarely as far north as southern Mexico. The nearest resident populations of Audubon's Shearwater in the Pacific are from eastern Polynesia (Marquesas, Tuamotu, and Pitcairn groups).

The Galápagos population of Audubon's Shearwater is large and does not seem to be seriously threatened. Nesting as they do in relatively inaccessible places, the shearwaters are less vulnerable than the Dark-rumped Petrel to predation by introduced mammals, other than man. Bones of Audubon's Shearwaters are common in many archaeological sites in Polynesia; this wide-ranging species has been, and in certain places unfortunately continues to be, an important food item of oceanic peoples.

PLATE 15

White-vented Storm-Petrel   *Oceanites gracilis*

Wedge-rumped Storm-Petrel   *Oceanodroma tethys*

The White-vented, or Elliot's Storm-Petrel (left) is the smallest of the three species of storm-petrels that live in the Galápagos. It is seen at sea within the Galápagos much more commonly than the others, slowly fluttering just above the ocean's surface, its dangling legs almost pattering along the water. These birds are daytime feeders on an abundance of small fish, shrimp, and plankton that thrive in the cool waters of the Humboldt and Peru currents.

The Galápagos population of the White-vented Storm-Petrel is regarded as a different race from the population that lives along the Pacific coast of South America. The Galápagos birds are somewhat larger than their relatives on the mainland, with a smaller area of white on their underside, and lighter overall coloration of their upperparts.

There is a major gap in our knowledge of the White-vented Storm-Petrel since its breeding grounds have never been found, either in the Galápagos or along the coast of South America. As a result, we know nothing about its nesting habits. The fact that the White-vented Storm-Petrels along the coast of South America differ in size and plumage from those in the Galápagos shows that two distinct breeding groups exist. The search for the nesting grounds of this species is somewhat complicated by its daily routine, for the White-vented Storm-Petrel feeds at sea by day and comes ashore only at night.

The Wedge-rumped, or Galápagos Storm-Petrel (right) also feeds on the abundant marine life of the Humboldt and

Peru currents. There are two distinct populations of Wedge-rumped Storm-Petrel, one of which nests in the Galápagos and the other on several islands off the coast of Peru. Three breeding colonies are known in the Galápagos: Isla Pitt, off the northern end of San Cristóbal; Genovesa; and Roca Redonda, off the northern coast of Isabela. The Wedge-rumped Storm-Petrel is seen at sea in the Galápagos less frequently than the White-vented Storm-Petrel, at least partly because much of its feeding at sea takes place at night.

Wedge-rumped Storm-Petrels in the Galápagos are larger and have longer wings than their relatives from coastal South America. The two populations of Wedge-rumped Storm-Petrels may mix, however; off the coast of Central and South America nonbreeding individuals of both races have been collected. If genetic interchange occurs between the two populations, as seems likely, this would explain why the Galápagos population of Wedge-rumped Storm-Petrels has evolved fewer differences from its mainland relatives than the White-vented Storm-Petrel has.

The size of the spectacular colony of Wedge-rumped Storm-Petrels on Genovesa has been estimated at up to 200,000 pairs. These birds are the staple diet of the Short-eared Owls living in the area. Yellow-crowned Night-Herons are also often seen in the storm-petrel colony, and occasionally may pluck a storm-petrel from a crack in the lava rock.

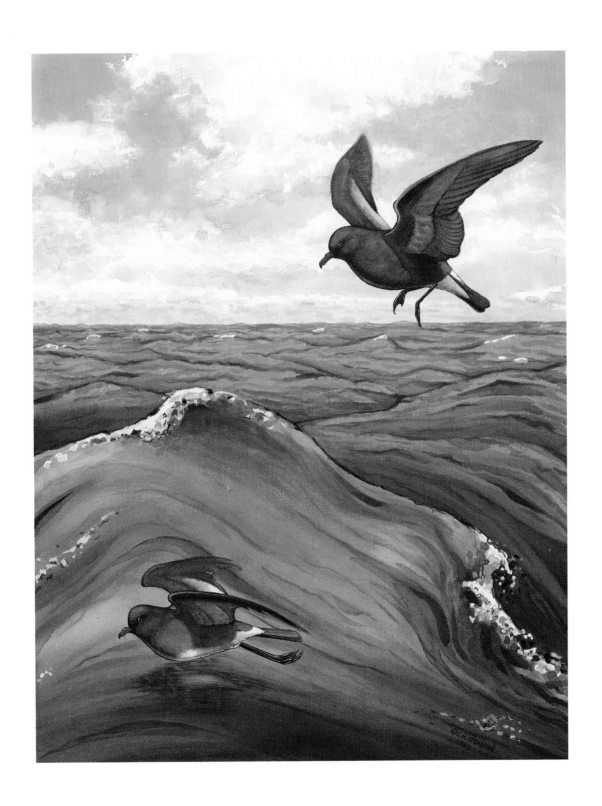

PLATE 16

Band-rumped Storm-Petrel *Oceanodroma castro*

The Band-rumped (Madeiran, or Harcourt's) Storm-Petrel is more widespread than the other two species of storm-petrels, both within and outside the Galápagos. There are about fifteen different nesting colonies of the Band-rumped Storm-Petrel in the islands. The species may be more common than one would guess from observations at sea in the Galápagos, for the Band-rumped Storm-Petrel feeds far offshore and thus is seldom observed by boats going from island to island.

The variation in Band-rumped Storm-Petrels has not been studied in detail. Outside of the Galápagos, they breed in subtropical waters of the North Pacific (Hawaii and Japan) and tropical and subtropical regions of the Atlantic. Nonbreeding birds have been recorded at sea from many places in the central and eastern Pacific. Presumably, most or all of the birds in the eastern Pacific are from the Galá-

pagos, and those from the central Pacific are from Hawaii, although this has not been documented.

The coexistence of three species of storm-petrels in the Galápagos can be explained by their different feeding habits. All three species feed on small fish, crustaceans, and cephalopods, but in different areas and at different times. The White-vented and Band-rumped Storm-Petrels feed by day, whereas the Wedge-rumped Storm-Petrel feeds mainly at night. Nearshore waters are used by the White-vented Storm-petrel, whereas the Wedge-rumped Storm-Petrel feeds both within Galápagos waters and over deeper water in all directions from the Galápagos. The feeding grounds of the Band-rumped Storm-Petrel are over deep water, in many cases farther offshore than those of the Wedge-rumped Storm-Petrel.

PLATE 17

Red-billed Tropicbird *Phaethon aethereus*

The Red-billed Tropicbird, a striking seabird that nests and roosts on cliffs overlooking the sea, is found in small, scattered groups nearly throughout the Galápagos, but in greater numbers where the ocean is relatively warm. Tropicbirds are as clumsy and helpless on land as they are graceful and skilled in the air. Their tiny legs and feet are positioned so far back on the body that walking or standing is impossible. Tropicbirds move awkwardly among their cliffside holes or along ledges by pushing with their feet while lying on their bellies. They nest on steep cliffs, from which they can take off by simply leaning forward into the air.

Although belonging to the order of birds that includes pelicans, cormorants, boobies, frigatebirds, and anhingas, the tropicbirds superficially resemble large terns in their appearance and habits, including diving for fish and squid. Like the other two species of tropicbirds, adults of the Red-billed Tropicbird have two greatly elongated central tail feathers, known as streamers. Sailors in former days thought these feathers resembled the marlin spikes carried by the boatswain and also associated the bird's whistle with the boatswain's pipe. Hence all species of tropicbirds became known as "boatswainbirds" or, among sailors, "bosunbirds."

The race of Red-billed Tropicbird in the Galápagos breeds in many other localities in the eastern Pacific and the Caribbean and in parts of the tropical Atlantic. The Galápagos race is relatively small, and the dark parts of its plumage are blacker. However, because of the similarity of the Galápagos population with those from other localities, either the Red-billed Tropicbird is a very recent colonizer of the islands or, as seems more likely, genetic exchange still takes place between the Galápagos birds and non-Galápagos populations. Red-billed Tropicbirds banded in the Galápagos have been recovered from coastal Panama and Peru, lending support to the second alternative.

While the Red-billed Tropicbird has generally escaped persecution by man, the White-tailed (or Yellow-billed) Tropicbird and the Red-tailed Tropicbird have been hunted by oceanic peoples for millennia. The eggs, juveniles, and adults have all been eaten as food, and the tail streamers—especially the long, striking ones of the Red-tailed Tropicbird—have been popular for adorning clothing and other objects. Bones of tropicbirds are fairly common in Polynesian archaeological sites, although I have never found a tropicbird fossil in the Galápagos. Because here the Red-billed Tropicbirds live exclusively on cliffs overlooking the sea, it is easy to see why bones would not be deposited by natural (nonhuman) means in the inland caves.

The excitement and pleasure of watching the Red-billed Tropicbird were described fifty years ago by Robert Cushman Murphy:

After weeks off soundings, in tropical blue waters where birds are scarce, the voyager may sometimes be electrified by hearing the shrill whistle of the Boatswain-bird. Looking aloft, he may see one, or perhaps a pair, of the gleaming, long-tailed creatures passing high in air on steadily and rapidly beating wings. On such occasions, according to my own experience, the visitors are likely to show a certain brief curiosity in the ship, and will turn off their courses in order to fly in an oval orbit around it once or twice before streaking away like animate comets. They are well named after Phaethon, the son of Apollo, who hurtled from the far sky into the sea. I remember the July day long ago when, at a point to eastward of Martinique but out of sight of land, I first saw one of a pair of Red-billed Tropicbirds dive from the height of the Daisy's masthead into the quiet, transparent water. For several seconds it remained below and, after reappearing, shook a shower of pearls from its feathers, rested at the surface with wings spread and raised, and tail plumes cocked up, and finally leaped into the air as lightly as a tern.

PLATE 18

Brown Pelican   *Pelecanus occidentalis*

Brown Noddy   *Anous stolidus*

The Brown Pelican is widely distributed along tropical and subtropical coastlines of the Americas. Armed with an elongated, pouched bill, the Brown Pelican dives for fish in shallow, coastal waters, but, being a less streamlined bird, its dives are less graceful and more splashy than those of boobies. The Brown Pelican builds a substantial nest of sticks overlooking the ocean, either on the ground or in bushes or small trees. Pelicans are seen commonly along the calmer shorelines of the Galápagos, flying alone or in small, single-file flocks. Often accompanied by frigatebirds, boobies, or gulls, the Brown Pelican regularly and aggressively follows incoming boats for scraps of cleaned fish.

The endemic Galápagos variety of Brown Pelican was described in 1945 by Alexander Wetmore, former Secretary of the Smithsonian Institution. The Galápagos race is darker than birds from mainland North and Central America in the Caribbean region, but is similar in coloration to those from the equatorial section of the Pacific coast from Colombia to northern Peru. What distinguishes it from birds of the last region (and those of the Caribbean as well) is its larger size. From northern Peru to southern Chile there is another race of the Brown Pelican, which is a good deal larger and lighter in color than either Galápagos birds or the coastal birds to the north. However, the Galápagos population of Brown Pelicans is most similar to the birds of the equatorial Pacific coast of South America, and we can therefore assume that the original colonization of the Galápagos probably came from this population.

The Brown Noddy is widespread in tropical seas. This distinctive species of tern is represented in the Galápagos by an endemic race. Compared with Brown Noddies from Polynesia, the Galápagos race is smaller, darker, and grayer in overall coloration. The Galápagos Brown Noddy is also darker than birds from the Pacific coast of Mexico, but of similar size. The light cap on the head is gray in the Galápagos birds, nearly pure white in those from Polynesia, and of intermediate color in the Mexican birds.

The nesting habits of the Brown Noddy also vary from place to place. In the Galápagos and in other rocky or cliffy regions, it usually nests in small crevices and holes or on ledges of seaside cliffs and caves. In much of Polynesia, the Brown Noddy often nests atop coconut palms, where it is vulnerable to predation by humans and rats that climb the trees.

The Brown Noddy is depicted here on the head of the Brown Pelican. This seemingly unusual habit, first noted by John James Audubon in the Caribbean, is actually common in the Galápagos and elsewhere. Edward Gifford once saw *two* noddies perched on a pelican's head. The pelican usually seems oblivious to the noddy's presence. I have observed a noddy perched on a pelican's head many times; presumably the noddy is waiting to grab small fish from the pelican's bill, but I have never witnessed any successful thievery. As part of its persistent search for food, the Brown Noddy will also follow small groups of Galápagos Penguins as they swim and dive for fish.

In spite of this habit of following other seabirds or schools of predatory fish to pilfer small fish on the surface, the presence of Brown Noddies at sea does not always indicate fish are nearby. On Mangaia in the Cook Islands, the natives told me that the Brown Noddy (called *ngoio* by the Mangaians) is not trusted by fishermen. While the Fairy Tern (*Gygis alba*) reliably indicates the presence of fish, the *ngoio* often leads the uninitiated angler into fishless water.

PLATE 19

Blue-footed Booby *Sula nebouxii*

The Blue-footed Booby may be the tourist's favorite seabird in the Galápagos. Its photogenic poses and expression, bright blue feet, extreme tameness (characteristic of all the boobies in the islands), and the unfortunate and undeserved connotation of stupidity in its name—combine to put this bird on center stage as a tourist attraction. Several of the boobies' nesting colonies are conveniently located along tourist trails, and their spectacular aerial dives, from heights of up to 80 feet, are readily observable and easily photographed. Probably more rolls of film are consumed on the Blue-footed Booby than on any other bird in the Galápagos.

The nest of the Blue-footed Booby is a shallow depression on bare ground from which most of the pebbles have been moved to the perimeter. Two or three eggs are laid in each nest, although generally only one or two of the hatchlings survive. The nesting cycle of the Blue-footed Booby is less seasonal than that of its relatives, the Masked and Red-footed Boobies. At nearly any time of year, active nests of the Blue-footed Booby can be found in the Galápagos. Often there is considerble variation within a single nesting colony, with some nests containing eggs and others hatchlings of various ages.

The Blue-footed Booby eats fish caught by diving underwater from on high. The boobies grasp the fish with their open bills rather than skewering them on closed bills. Ornithologists A. K. Fisher and Alexander Wetmore, on a visit to the islands in 1931, wrote an excellent description of the dive of the Blue-footed Booby:

One never tires of watching this and other species of the family diving for fish. With wings tightly pressed against the body the birds descend at an angle of 45° like a projectile, often from considerable heights, striking the water with a thud and reappearing at the surface 8 or 10 feet beyond as if following a parabolic curve. One afternoon at Wreck Bay, Chatham Island [San Cristóbal], five boobies of this species gave a fine exhibition, descending in almost perfect alignment to strike the water and reappear together. After a moment's rest they arose in a half spiral to regain position for another onslaught on their prey. This maneuvering over a rather restricted area was kept up for fully half an hour.

Unlike the Masked or the Red-footed Booby, the Blue-footed Booby is seldom seen far at sea. It forages by preference in relatively shallow coastal waters. The fact that this species does not stray far from the islands and thus has little or no genetic contact with the birds of the mainland coast, helps explain why the Galápagos race has evolved differences from its mainland cousins.

PLATE 20

Masked Booby   *Sula dactylatra*

The Masked Booby occurs in tropical seas around the world. Other names for this largest of living boobies are White Booby and Blue-faced Booby. The Masked Booby nests in colonies scattered throughout the Galápagos and is often associated with either the Blue-footed or Red-footed Booby, but almost never with both. These three species are seldom seen together at sea, for the Blue-footed Booby feeds in shallow water near shore, the Masked Booby in deeper water offshore, and the Red-footed Booby even farther offshore.

The subspecies of Masked Booby in the Galápagos is found on other islands in the eastern Pacific from Mexico to Ecuador, with an outlying colony on San Felix and San Ambrosio islands, well off northern Chile. Much like the Red-billed Tropicbird, the Masked Booby population in the Galápagos probably has regular genetic contact with individuals from outside the archipelago. There is some evidence that the colors of the bill and feet differ in the Galápagos birds, but these colors vary with age and sex and are thus difficult to study and evaluate over the entire range of the species.

The Masked Booby nests on the ground in a shallow, rather featureless scrape similar to that of the Blue-footed Booby. One or two eggs are laid, but almost without exception, only one chick survives per nest. The Masked Booby, although rightly considered a bird of tropical seas, suffered badly in the Galápagos during the extremely warm waters of the 1982–83 El Niño. Throughout the archipelago, few if any chicks survived, and only a few individual adults were seen where normally there were massive colonies. Most of the adults left for more lucrative fishing grounds and did not return to nest or attempt to raise young. Robert Cushman Murphy noted that:

On the Pacific Coast of South America, this White [Masked] Booby is one of the species which serves as an index of the advancing water of the [warm] countercurrent from the north. It is unknown in the zone of normal upwelling along the shores of Peru, but, during influxes of El Niño between December and April, examples frequently fly southward past Point Parinas, so that the oceanic range of the species comes to overlap that of the normal birdlife of the Humboldt Current. Such vagaries are not to be wondered at, because the distribution of flying fishes undergoes this same extension during the same periods.

The Masked Booby's taste for flying fish is strong. The lighthouse keeper on Isla La Plata, just off Ecuador, told Murphy that his fishing bait consisted exclusively of regurgitated flying fish, obtained by tickling the throats of Masked Boobies with a switch.

PLATE 21

Red-footed Booby *Sula sula*

The Red-footed Booby is widespread in tropical oceans. In the Galápagos, this smallest of living boobies nests only in five colonies at the periphery of the archipelago. The Red-footed Booby feeds in deep water far offshore, and is thus encountered at sea within the Galápagos less frequently than the Blue-footed or Masked Boobies.

The race of Red-footed Booby in the Galápagos also breeds on the Revilla Gigedo Islands and Clipperton Islands off Mexico and on Cocos Island, between Costa Rica and the Galápagos. The Red-footed Booby's preference for foraging far offshore probably explains why it does not breed on the numerous Pacific coastal islands from Mexico through South America.

In the Galápagos, as elsewhere, the Red-footed Booby occurs in two distinct color phases, a brown phase and a white phase. Lee has painted a nesting pair of Red-footed Boobies consisting of one bird of each color phase; this is not uncommon since the birds themselves show no particular color preference in choosing their mates. Furthermore, some birds are bicolored, basically brown but with symmetrical white patches here and there. The proportion of brown-versus-white birds varies from place to place, with brown birds outnumbering white birds in most localities. In the Galápagos, only about 5 percent of the Red-footed Boobies are white.

The estimated 140,000 pairs of Red-footed Boobies on Genovesa form a major part of one of the world's largest seabird concentrations. These tame birds nest in trees and bushes and are easy to observe at close range. It is obvious how vulnerable these and other boobies would be to human predation if anyone were so inclined. While the idea of eating a booby probably (and hopefully) does not seem appealing, I have identified hundreds of bones of Red-footed and Masked Boobies as well as Brown Boobies (*Sula leucogaster*) from the kitchen middens of prehistoric Polynesians on Pacific islands where boobies were a regular part of the menu. The Red-footed Booby has declined in range and numbers throughout the Pacific because of human intrusions of one kind or another. The long-term survival of this booby may well depend on maintenance of such protected, natural refuges as Genovesa.

Only one other species of booby nests in trees. This is the endangered Abbott's Booby (*Papasula abbotti*), found only on Christmas Island in the eastern Indian Ocean, where it nests high in native forests. Very recently, coworkers Dominique Pahlavan, Susan Schubel, and I discovered bones of Abbott's Booby from a prehistoric kitchen midden on Tikopia in the Solomon Islands, some 3,000 miles east of Christmas Island. Even more surprising was our discovery of bones of a larger, closely related species of booby from kitchen middens in the Marquesas Islands, more than 5,000 miles east of Christmas Island. We named this extinct species "Costello's Booby" to complement Abbott's Booby. Considering the likelihood that Abbott's and Costello's Boobies were once found through much of the Pacific, oceanic peoples probably have destroyed hundreds of thousands of these birds—yet another reason to be grateful for the protection of boobies in the Galápagos.

PLATE 22

Flightless Cormorant *Phalacrocorax harrisi*

The Flightless Cormorant is one of the most famous sea-birds of the Galápagos, although astonishingly it was not formally described before the Webster-Harris Expedition of 1897. Cormorant colonies are restricted to the shores of Isabela and Fernandina, and the birds seldom stray inland more than a few yards.

The Flightless Cormorant has been said to be the only living cormorant that has lost the ability to fly, making the bird of special interest to scientists and conservationists. Yet while dangers to this species and to the Galápagos Penguin from human intrusion exist, the most serious threat to populations of both birds is the possibility of widespread starvation should a major and prolonged El Niño result in a catastrophic reduction of their marine food supplies. In 1982–83 large numbers of birds of both species died and few survivors had the strength to reproduce. However, these birds have shown remarkable powers of recovery. Their populations have now been restored, and we can conclude that it would take a prolonged period or series of El Niño's to threaten them with total extermination.

Mainly because of similarities in plumage, I believe the Galápagos Flightless Cormorant may have evolved from an early colonization of the islands by the Double-crested Cormorant (*Phalacrocorax auritus*) or its Pleistocene counterpart. The nesting range of the Double-crested Cormorant along the Pacific coast extends from Alaska south through Baja California. Outside of the nesting season, this migratory species has been recorded as far south as southern Mexico, various West Indian islands, and far offshore in Bermuda.

I have two different theories about the original colonization of the Galápagos cormorants. The first is that it occurred from the north during a glacial interval. During the times of major advances of continental ice sheets, the Double-crested Cormorant probably ranged farther south than today, both as a breeding bird and as a migrant. Once in the Galápagos, the abundance of food, combined with a relaxation of migratory habits and a lack of mammalian predators, eliminated the need to fly. Eventually, natural selection favored extremely well-developed legs and feet for swimming and diving.

The second theory suggests that the Flightless Cormorant may have evolved on the Pacific coast of South America. The discovery of cormorant fossils in the Galápagos or in coastal South America will help determine whether either of these theories can account for the bird we know today in the islands.

PLATE 23

Great Frigatebird *Fregata minor*

The Great Frigatebird is abundant and widespread in the tropical Pacific and Indian oceans and also occurs, though much less commonly, in the South Atlantic. It is common and conspicuous in the Galápagos. The name "Great" Frigatebird is hardly appropriate, for the species actually is slightly smaller than its near relative, the Magnificent Frigatebird (*Fregata magnificens*), which also resides in the islands. The males of the two species found in the Galápagos are very similar in overall appearance and behavior, although the black plumage of the male Great Frigatebirds (bottom) has an iridescent green sheen, whereas the Magnificent Frigatebird has an iridescent purple sheen. The females are easier to distinguish: females of the Great Frigatebird (top) have a red eye ring and a white throat; female Magnificent Frigatebirds have a blue eye ring and a black throat. Finally, juvenile Great Frigatebirds have an orangy tinge on the head and neck, but their heads become all white after their first molt, and they may then be indistinguishable in the field from their Magnificent relatives. Like the Red-footed Booby, the Great Frigatebird is represented in the Galápagos by a race that also breeds on the Revilla Gigedo Islands, off Mexico, and on Cocos Island, between the Galápagos and Costa Rica.

All species of frigatebirds are also known as "man-of-war birds" or "man-o'-war birds" because of their piratic feeding habits. A. K. Fisher and Alexander Wetmore made these observations of Great Frigatebirds on Genovesa:

In feeding habits they have two very dissimilar methods of procuring food, namely, as robbers and as scavengers. As pirates they rob other birds of fish just captured, and as scavengers they pick morsels from the ocean surface. When taking food from the water the wing tips are thrown upward with wonderful grace as the bird poises for a moment, while reaching downward with extended neck. The booby appears to be the most frequent victim upon which these great birds practice piracy. When boobies find shoals of fish and are feeding in numbers, the man-o'-war birds are sure to be hovering near to secure their unjust share of the chase. Some individual boobies seem to have acquired prudence, and after catching fish, remain on the surface long enough to be forgotten by their persecutors before taking wing to resume their pursuit of food. The man-o'-war bird also robs the noddy, and at times pursues the little stormy petrel.

Genovesa is probably the world's best place to observe Great Frigatebirds. Anchored in Darwin Bay, you can watch them pilfer food from other seabirds. Walking along the main tourist trail just behind the beach, tens to hundreds may be seen at their nests, either displaying, incubating eggs, or feeding young. Lee has painted a male and female that have just paired up. The gaudy, bright red throat sac of the male is inflated to attract the white-throated female.

PLATE 24

Magnificent Frigatebird *Fregata magnificens*

A second species of avian pirate, the Magnificent Frigatebird, resides in the Galápagos. In this plate a female (left) and male (right) are perched, while an immature glides overhead. The Magnificent Frigatebird is generally found close to continental coasts and adjacent islands, whereas the Great Frigatebird is confined to oceanic islands. The Galápagos Islands are the only place where these two species co-exist (though in much of the South Pacific, the Great Frigatebird co-exists with the Lesser Frigatebird, *Fregata ariel*). The conditions that permit the cohabitation of the Galápagos by two such similar species of frigatebirds are poorly understood by scientists. It would be interesting to learn if these two species differ much in their feeding habits. Most nesting colonies are strictly of one species or the other; the Great Frigatebirds tend to be found in the outlying parts of the archipelago, while Magnificent Frigatebirds are found more commonly on the larger, central islands.

Throughout their range in the subtropical and tropical Atlantic, eastern Pacific, and Caribbean, Magnificent Frigatebirds all look fairly similar. Although it is a marine species, the bird is regularly observed flying over continental areas near shore. Interbreeding between the Pacific and Caribbean populations probably occurs regularly, for these birds are seen over land in Central America, especially during storms. Some years ago, while studying the feeding and nesting habits of the Ocellated Turkey (*Meleagris ocellata*) at the Mayan archaeological site of Tikal, Guatemala, I was astonished to see a Magnificent Frigatebird soaring overhead during an April storm. In a setting of Mayan pyramids surrounded by tall tropical forests, this bird seemed extremely out of place.

PLATE 25

American Oystercatcher *Haematopus palliatus*

Lava Gull *Larus fuliginosus*

The American Oystercatcher (left) is found along seacoasts of the West Indies and of North, Central, and South America, including Colombia, Ecuador, Peru, and Chile. The endemic race of American Oystercatcher in the Galápagos may be distinguished from other races by its darker back color and by having less white in the wing feathers. These differences are well suited for foraging along Galápagos seashores, where the oystercatcher's dark color blends well with the lava rocks, making it less visible to some of the animals on which it preys. Even the seemingly conspicuous red bill often escapes notice unless you are very near.

Within the islands American Oystercatchers are widespread but not abundant. They are most commonly seen in small family groups of two or three birds along a beach or rocky coastline. Oystercatchers almost never stray inland, since the animals they eat live only in the intertidal zone. In temperate regions, oystercatchers consume a variety of shellfish, especially their namesake, oysters. In the Galápagos, as well as in some other tropical regions, oystercatchers are less selective in their food preferences, feeding on chitons, limpets, small crabs, sea slugs, and other intertidal invertebrates.

Galápagos oystercatchers are extremely tame compared with those of the mainland. Subjected to predation by no native mammals and few if any birds, they allow you to approach closely as long as you are slow and quiet. The adult painted here by Lee is standing next to a Lava Gull, a common seaside associate.

The Lava Gull (right) is found only in the Galápagos, where it is widespread though not abundant. Its preferred habitat is along the beaches, whereas the cliffs and rocky shores are home to the other Galápagos gull, the Swallow-tailed Gull. Lava Gulls scavenge scraps of fish or meat on the shore or in the water, and will sometimes steal fish from other seabirds.

Because the Lava Gull is an endemic species, its evolutionary history has been lost in the distant past. It is most closely related to the Laughing Gull (*Larus atricilla*), a common and widespread coastal species of North, Central, and South America, which also strays to the islands. The pattern of juvenile and adult plumages is practically identical in the Lava Gull and Laughing Gull. The main difference is that the Lava Gull is darker in overall coloration, a distinction characteristic of other Galápagos seashore birds such as the American Oystercatcher, Great Blue Heron, Lava Heron, and Yellow-crowned Night-Heron.

Lava and Laughing Gulls are both scavengers along seashores and shallow waters. Even the long, loud, cackling call from which the Laughing Gull gets its name is characteristic of both species. Ornithologist Edward Gifford, in his report for the California Academy of Sciences Expedition, described this call as "beginning with a chuckle and then breaking into a cackling laugh."

Some time in the not-too-distant past, perhaps only some thousands or tens of thousands of years ago, a group of Laughing Gulls colonized the Galápagos, remained, and reproduced. The resulting Lava Gull is still as similar to the modern Laughing Gull as the Lava Heron is to the Striated Heron, or the dark race of Yellow-crowned Night-Heron to its mainland counterpart. Interbreeding between Lava Gulls and visiting Laughing Gulls may still take place.

PLATE 26

Swallow-tailed Gull *Larus furcatus*

The graceful Swallow-tailed Gull (adult above, immature below) is a dazzling bird to see on the wing. With its brightly patterned head and wings, and a forked tail of bright white, this gull is often said to be endemic to the Galápagos, although there is a breeding population on Malpelo Island off Colombia. Unlike the resident and sedentary Lava Gull, the Swallow-tailed Gull is seen regularly off the coasts of Panama, Colombia, Ecuador, and Peru. Many of these birds probably are from the Galápagos rather than Malpelo. In April 1982 I saw several Swallow-tailed Gulls far out at sea, halfway between the Galápagos and the mainland.

The Swallow-tailed Gull differs from the Lava Gull in its habits and habitat as well as appearance. It is not a shoreline scavenger, but feeds by night at sea on squid and perhaps small fish. It prefers a rocky habitat and nests and roosts on seaside cliffs in loose congregations that may number in the hundreds or thousands.

The origin of the Swallow-tailed Gull is an evolutionary curiosity. Interestingly enough, its nearest relative is Sabine's Gull (*Larus sabini*), a smaller species that only nests north of the Arctic Circle. The plumages of these two species are very similar in color and pattern, including the distinctive wing pattern and the forked tail, and both differ significantly in these respects from all other species of gulls. Both Swallow-tailed and Sabine's Gulls also have a red eye ring and a black bill tipped with yellow.

Although Sabine's Gulls nest only in the high Arctic, they are highly migratory and pelagic at other seasons. A significant portion of the world population winters in the equatorial eastern Pacific, and numbers of them are seen annually in the general region of the Galápagos. Thus it seems very likely that Swallow-tailed Gulls evolved in the Galápagos from an early colonization by a group of Sabine's Gulls that began to feed and roost in the islands and failed to return to their Arctic homelands.

PLATE 27

Sooty Tern *Sterna fuscata*

The Sooty Tern ranges widely throughout all tropical oceans of the world. It is easily recognized, being the only Pacific tern that has a dark (sooty black) back and white underparts. Within the Galápagos, there are sizable colonies of Sooty Terns on Culpepper Island where oceanic conditions are relatively warm. They are unknown in the cool waters of coastal Ecuador and Peru.

The Galápagos race of Sooty Tern is also found on various islands off the Pacific coast of Mexico and Panama, although it is not known if these populations interbreed. Other races are found in the Caribbean and in Polynesia. The underparts of the Galápagos terns are grayer than in the Caribbean birds, and the tail is shorter and darker than that of Polynesian terns.

Except in nesting season, Sooty Terns spend most of their time over the open sea. They take their prey from the surface rather than diving as many other terns do, since their feathers are not waterproof and would quickly become waterlogged. This raises the interesting question of where and how Sooty Terns sleep. At least one authority has speculated that they do their sleeping on the wing.

The distribution of Sooty Terns, both within and outside of the Galápagos, is highly dependent on oceanic conditions. If the islands became slightly cooler, the Sooty Tern would be in trouble, even on the northern outpost of Culpepper. On the other hand, a long-term warming trend might stimulate Sooty Terns to colonize additional islands in the Galápagos. This is just the opposite of the situation with Galápagos Penguins or Flightless Cormorants, whose existence depends on cool waters rather than warm. The future of Sooty Terns also depends, in the Galápagos and elsewhere, on nesting islands that are free of rats.

PLATE 28

Great Blue Heron *Ardea herodias*

This large, conspicuous heron is familiar to most Americans. It nests throughout North America from Alaska through much of Mexico and the West Indies, and south to Panama, Colombia, and Venezuela. Nonbreeding birds are widespread in Central America and northern South America. An endemic race of Great Blue Heron resides in the Galápagos, where the species is well dispersed but not abundant. The Galápagos race is darker in overall coloration than mainland birds.

Great Blue Herons are usually solitary in the Galápagos where they are not known to roost or nest in rookeries as their mainland counterparts do. While preferring a diet of fish, they are opportunistic feeders and dine on what they can catch. Unlike mainland Great Blue Herons, they show no preference for fresh water but do their foraging in the intertidal zone and in brackish lagoons. Like other species of herons in the Galápagos, the Great Blue Heron nests mainly or exclusively in mangrove trees.

Great Blue Herons are very tame in the Galápagos. For years, one particularly amiable Great Blue Heron showed up every day at a seaside hotel in Puerto Ayora (the village near the Darwin Station) where it stalked among guests at tables, and accepted scraps of meat and fish as its customary due.

I grew up with Great Blue Herons. Every year from April through October, one or two birds visited our farm ponds in Pennsylvania on a daily routine. Still my most memorable incident with a Great Blue Heron occurred in the Galápagos and involved the very heron depicted in this plate. While visiting Fernandina in May 1983, I watched a Great Blue Heron seize a young marine iguana with its bill. Against the background of an angry El Niño sky, the heron shook the iguana vigorously for about five minutes. Then, craning its neck skyward and gulping violently, the heron finally managed to swallow its large victim, although for some time the heron's neck remained visibly swollen.

PLATE 29

Great Egret   *Ardea alba*

Common Gallinule   *Gallinula chloropus*

The Great Egret (left), known also as the Common Egret, American Egret, Large Egret, or White Egret, is distributed through most temperate and tropical regions of the world. A single race is found throughout the Americas, including the Galápagos. We see occasional Great Egrets searching for finny prey in the calm, saline lagoons, but they are not abundant in the islands and stray inland only occasionally and briefly. Like Galápagos Great Blue Herons, Great Egrets are relatively solitary. They are usually seen singly or in pairs, and they neither roost nor nest in rookeries as their relatives on the mainland do. While the Great Egret probably hunts the same sort of prey as the Great Blue Heron, neither species is numerous enough in the Galápagos to cause significant interspecies competition.

Unlike most species of Galápagos birds, the Great Egret is wary of humans. This fact, along with the lack of anatomical differences between the islands' birds and those of the mainland, leads me to believe that Great Egrets are relatively recent colonizers.

The Common Gallinule (right), also called the Common Moorhen, is an aquatic species of rail that is found nearly worldwide. It is common throughout Central America and in much of South America, including the coast of Ecuador and Peru. Whether a distinct race of Common Gallinule resides in the Galápagos has not been conclusively determined, but the Galápagos birds closely resemble those from Central America as well as those from coastal Ecuador and Peru.

Like the Great Egret, I suspect that Common Gallinules also colonized the Galápagos relatively recently. They too are anatomically similar to their relatives on the mainland and are unusually wary and shy for Galápagos species.

The Great Egret and the Common Gallinule are depicted together in this plate since the two species share similar habitat preferences. Both are usually found along the edges of mangrove-lined saline pools near the coast, although gallinules can occasionally be seen in the freshwater pools of the highlands.

PLATE 30

Lava Heron   *Ardeola sundevalli*

Striated Heron   *Ardeola striata*

These two herons present a taxonomic riddle, for scientists have not determined whether they are distinct species or merely different color phases of the same species. The endemic Lava Heron (above), also known as the Plumbeous Heron, is found fairly commonly throughout the Galápagos. The Striated Heron (below), considered by some ornithologists to be the same species as the familiar Green Heron of North America, has been recorded in the Galápagos only from San Cristóbal, Santa Cruz, Pinzón, Isabela, Fernandina, and Pinta. Striated Herons are widespread in aquatic habitats of tropical South America, including the Pacific coasts of Colombia, Ecuador, and Peru. No one has ever reported the nest of a Striated Heron in the Galápagos, although it is presumably a permanent resident like the Lava Heron.

There is little doubt that the Lava Heron evolved from the Striated Heron. The two species are highly similar in size, shape, and general habits. In the Galápagos, both are found only along the coast. The slightly larger bill of the Lava Heron is probably an adaptation for eating crabs. Crouched and extremely alert, Lava Herons stalk the Galápagos shorelines for shrimp, small fish, and especially crabs. Unlike the colorful Striated Heron, the plumage of the Lava Heron is mainly shades of dark gray, well adapted for life on the rocky shorelines of the Galápagos, where it is even less evident to its prey than the Galápagos races of American Oystercatchers or Yellow-crowned Night-Herons.

It is interesting to speculate whether the Lava Heron and Striated Heron are separate species that colonized the Galápagos on two separate occasions, or whether they offer a living example of evolution in action. Most Galápagos individuals are of the Lava Heron type (with dark plumage), yet a few still retain the colorful plumage of the ancestral Striated Heron. A key question, for which no one has yet provided the answer, is whether the two species interbreed. My own opinion is that they probably do, since the plumage of the Lava Heron is not uniform. Certain individuals have regions of white or light gray feathers on the throat, neck, breast, or beneath the tail, which leads me to believe that the ancestral plumage of the Striated Heron is gradually being replaced by the better camouflaged plumage of the Lava Heron.

© LEE MARC STEADMAN
1987

PLATE 31

Yellow-Crowned Night-Heron *Nyctanassa violacea*

Resting on a mangrove-lined seashore, the immature (left) and adult (right) Yellow-crowned Night-Herons that Lee has portrayed in this painting give the impression of being very stoic birds. Yellow-crowned Night-Herons are common residents in much of North and Central America and the West Indies. In South America, they are found mainly along the coasts, from Colombia through northern Peru. The endemic Galápagos race of Yellow-crowned Night-Heron is smaller and, like several of the seaside birds of the Galápagos, darker in overall coloration than its mainland relatives.

Within the Galápagos, the Yellow-crowned Night-Heron is widespread, fairly common, and most often solitary, although now and then two or three birds may be seen together. These extremely tame herons are usually found along rocky or cliffy shorelines or in mangrove-lined lagoons, although they can be found inland more often than other local herons and have been seen at 2,400-feet elevation on Volcan Alcedo, Isabela. Yellow-crowned Night-Herons are accomplished runners; some observers have even compared them with roadrunners as they pursue grasshoppers and similar prey on land. Crabs are their preferred food along the shore, but they regularly forage for large insects in upland habitats. I have seen these herons hunting for grasshoppers in thorny forest on Santa Cruz, two miles inland from Academy Bay, and I suspect that they also take lizards, rodents, and small birds once in a while.

PLATE 32

Black Rail *Laterallus jamaicensis*

The Galápagos variety of Black Rail has also been called the Galápagos Rail, Galápagos Black Rail, or Darwin's Rail. The Black Rail is found very locally in marshes from North America through Central America and along the Pacific coast of South America to central Chile. This sparrow-sized, inconspicuous swamp-dweller is extremely difficult to observe in its mainland habitats, and very little is known of its habits there. Black Rails are migratory in the northern part of their continental range. Tropical forms, including those in the Galápagos, are not migratory.

The endemic Galápagos race of Black Rail has been recorded from San Cristóbal, Floreana, Santa Cruz, Baltra, Santiago, Pinta, Isabela, and Fernandina. On the average, Galápagos birds differ from mainland varieties in their paler heads, a reduced amount of white spotting on the wings and white barring on the underparts, larger bill and feet, and shorter tail. In the 1800s and early 1900s, the Black Rail was found in coastal mangrove swamps as well as in the humid highlands of the Galápagos. For at least several decades, however, they have not been found along the coasts, although no one has been able to explain why.

Black Rails are common today in many localities in the highlands. Santa Cruz, for example, supports what must be the world's densest population of Black Rails. Lurking in the island's thick areas of ferns, grasses, and sedges, these tiny, tame rails are not at all difficult to find, although—as with most rails anywhere—they are easier to hear than to see. Nevertheless, by sitting still and imitating their call (either by hitting two stones together or by cheating with a tape recorder), Black Rails will nearly walk over your feet. This has happened to me numerous times on Santa Cruz, especially on Devine's cattle ranch. Seeing the birds airborne is a different matter. Except for purposes of migration, Black Rails everywhere are reluctant to fly, depending instead on their ability to slip away and hide in the thick cover they inhabit.

PLATE 33

Paint-billed Crake *Neocrex erythrops*

This rail is appropriately named for its bright red and yellow bill. It shares the humid highlands of the Galápagos with the smaller Black Rail. (The names "rail" and "crake" are basically synonymous, although rail is a better generic term for any species in the family.) The Paint-billed Crake is also found in tropical South America, including a population along the Pacific coast of Peru. The Galápagos form is believed to be identical to the continental birds, although detailed comparisons have not been made. Paint-billed Crakes reside in the Galápagos on San Cristóbal, Floreana, Santa Cruz, and Isabela, with a single record from Genovesa.

There is little doubt that the Paint-billed Crake is a recent colonizer of the Galápagos. It was first discovered here only in 1953. Based on records of the past few decades, this species seems to be increasing its range and numbers within the archipelago. In the highland ranch country of Santa Cruz, the Paint-billed Crake is just as common today as the Black Rail. It is likely that Paint-billed Crakes will be reported soon from other islands in the Galápagos.

Paint-billed Crakes are more willing to fly than Black Rails. It is interesting to note that of the three species of rails that have colonized the Galápagos—the Common Gallinule, Black Rail, and Paint-billed Crake—none has evolved flightless forms. This seems a little strange because flightless rails are one of the most characteristic types of insular birds. Islands much more remote than the Galápagos, such as St. Helena, Ascension, the Hawaiian Islands, and Wake, have all been colonized by rails that subsequently lost the ability to fly. In Polynesia alone, hundreds or thousands of populations existed before people colonized the islands.

Unfortunately, nearly all flightless rails are extinct today, victims of human intervention.

Storrs Olson of the Smithsonian Institution, an authority on flightless rails, has pointed out that flightlessness evolves very rapidly in island rails, perhaps to conserve energy by reducing the size of the wing and breast muscles. So why have no species of rails become flightless in the Galápagos Islands?

One factor is probably the type of rail. Most of the flightless species belong to one of several generic groups of rails that appear to be more prone to flightlessness than those that have colonized the Galápagos.

A second factor is time. The Galápagos populations of Common Gallinule and Paint-billed Crake are anatomically the same as populations from elsewhere, and thus these two species probably have resided in the Galápagos for too short a period of time for such a radical evolutionary process to have developed. The Black Rail, however, has lived in the Galápagos long enough to evolve differences in size and plumage. Its reluctance to fly is very characteristic, yet it has not become flightless.

A third factor may be the need of these species to fly to escape predatory mammals. Most species of flightless rails evolved on islands that lacked terrestrial mammals. Until recently, many Galápagos islands were inhabited by native rodents. It may be that these native rodents, perhaps especially the extinct giant rats of Santa Cruz and Isabela, preyed on ground-dwelling birds to some extent. Such predation may have inhibited natural selection toward flightlessness.

PLATE 34

Common Stilt   *Himantopus himantopus*

White-cheeked Pintail   *Anas bahamensis*

These two aquatic species are often found together in brackish lagoons in the Galápagos. The Common Stilt (left), also known as the Black-necked Stilt, wades through calm, shallow water on extremely long and thin legs. It is found in southern and western North America, the Hawaiian Islands, the West Indies, Central America, and much of South America, including the Pacific coast of Peru and Chile. Other races of this species are found in the Old World.

The race of Common Stilt in the Galápagos is identical to the widespread form in North, Central, and South America. This suggests that stilts arrived in the Galápagos fairly recently. Common Stilts on the continent, in the West Indies, or in Hawaii can be found regularly in either fresh water or saline habitats, but in the Galápagos they are only seen in the brackish lagoons. Stilts are fairly widespread in the Galápagos, although seldom in flocks of more than a dozen or so.

An exception occurred, however, during the 1982–83 El Niño. On Baltra I was astonished to see how the torrential rains had transformed this normally parched and brown island into a steaming thicket of green vegetation.

Hundreds of fresh water pools dotted the landscape of an island that ordinarily lacks any fresh water. In these pools were hundreds of Common Stilts and White-cheeked Pintails; the floods of El Niño had flushed out many of the coastal lagoons they typically occupy.

The White-cheeked Pintail (right), often called the Bahamas Pintail or the Bahamas Duck, is a rather small duck that is found through much of tropical America, including coastal Ecuador and Peru. Compared with members of the species found in South America and the West Indies, the endemic Galápagos race of White-cheeked Pintail is smaller and darker. Also, in the Galápagos variety the white cheek blends more gradually with the brown color of the rest of the head.

As with other endemic races, the White-cheeked Pintail is much tamer in the Galápagos than elsewhere. In the West Indies, for example, these long-hunted birds have retreated to the most inaccessible wetlands, where they are shy and wary. The White-cheeked Pintail is still fairly common in the Galápagos and may be readily observed as it paddles unconcernedly across brackish pools and inland lakes—as it once must have done in the West Indies as well.

PLATE 35

Greater Flamingo   *Phoenicopterus ruber*

Various species and subspecies of this majestic pink bird are found in southern Europe, much of Africa, the Middle East and southern Russia through India, and the Americas. In the New World the Greater Flamingo, sometimes called the American Flamingo, may be found in Yucatan, the West Indies, and the Caribbean and Atlantic coasts of South America from Colombia to northern Brazil. The endemic race of Greater Flamingo in the Galápagos differs from mainland species in its paler overall coloration, slightly different shape of bill, and slightly shorter neck, wing, and tarsus.

An estimated two hundred to four hundred flamingos are scattered throughout the islands, where they occur in colonies of ten to one hundred birds. They inhabit the salty lagoons along the coast, together with gallinules, stilts, pintails, herons, and egrets. Remarkably, flamingo populations in the Galápagos were not severely reduced during the 1982–83 El Niño. Much fresh water poured into their lagoons, and the red organic ooze on which these filter-feeding birds subsist became exceedingly scarce. In addition, many flamingo nesting sites were drowned out by rising water levels. The flamingos persisted, however, and with the restoration of "normal" conditions their numbers are about where they were before El Niño.

The flamingo depicted here by Lee lived on Rábida during our visit in 1984. Day in and day out, this bird and several companions fed in the lagoon, methodically sweeping their bills from side to side as they filtered out microorganisms from the rich waters.

Although wary by comparison with many Galápagos birds, the flamingos in the islands are extremely tame compared with those of other localities. If you are quiet and move slowly, it is easy to approach within 50 or 100 feet of this regal bird.

PLATE 36

Galápagos Hawk   *Buteo galapagoensis*

The Galápagos Hawk is an endemic species once found in all of the main islands in the archipelago except Genovesa, Wenman, and Culpepper. However, Galápagos farmers have persecuted this bird mercilessly, believing it to be a threat to their chickens. Today it is absent or extremely rare on San Cristóbal, Floreana, and Baltra, as well as on the small islands of North Seymour and Daphne. Even on Santa Cruz, it has become rare over the past few decades.

Like many other species of hawks, the evolution of the Galápagos bird is poorly understood. No one has ever compared its internal anatomy with that of other species, and its plumage, while somewhat better studied, is difficult to interpret in evolutionary terms. The Galápagos Hawk has a distinctive immature plumage, mainly a mottled combination of brown and white, as depicted in the bird in the lower left of this plate. The adult, shown on the right, is largely dark grayish brown over the entire body, with a tail patterned in different shades of gray.

The adult plumage of the Galápagos Hawk is extremely similar in color and pattern to the dark-phase adult plumage of Swainson's Hawk (*Buteo swainsoni*). Likewise, the immature plumage of the Galápagos Hawk is nearly identical to that of certain immature individuals of Swainson's Hawk. Although these similarities suggest a close relationship between these two species, another mainland species, the Red-backed Hawk (*Buteo polyosoma*), also closely resembles the Galápagos Hawk in both immature and adult plumages.

Geographically, both Swainson's Hawk and the Red-backed Hawk are eligible to be the closest relatives of the Galápagos Hawk. The Red-backed Hawk is a widespread tropical species, not uncommon along the coasts of Ecuador and Peru. Swainson's Hawk nests only in western North America (from Mexico to Alaska), but in winter huge flocks migrate annually to Central America and northern South America, including the coasts of Ecuador and Peru.

This migratory and flocking behavior might have made Swainson's Hawk a more likely candidate for the colonization of new regions than the local and sedentary Red-backed Hawk. It does not seem farfetched to suggest that a flock of migrant Swainson's Hawks was blown seaward, found a landfall in the Galápagos, and established a colony there—the descendants of which in time evolved into the Galápagos Hawk. It was from just such a colonization by migrant Sabine's Gulls that we believe Swallow-tailed Gulls developed in the islands. However, thorough study and comparison of plumages and feeding habits of all three species is needed before any definitive conclusion can be reached about the ancestry of the Galápagos Hawk—or why it has larger feet and claws than either of its suspected progenitors.

Finally, I must mention the remarkable tameness of Galápagos Hawks. The two painted here by Lee were a regular part of our camp scene on Volcan Wolf, Isabela, in 1984. The immature hawk was particularly tame, and often hovered within inches of our heads as we explored the volcanic slopes. On Fernandina in 1980, I watched in amazement as *five* Galápagos Hawks perched on André DeRoy's head and shoulders, while others circled nearby, looking for perches of their own. André's whistling had a sort of "Pied Piper" effect on the hawks. For those of us conditioned to the skittish nature of continental hawks, the sight of untrained, "wild" hawks perched on a person seemed altogether incredible.

PLATE 37

Galápagos Dove   *Zenaida galapagoensis*

The Galápagos Dove is one of the most widespread species of land birds in the archipelago. It resides on every major island, although the populations from San Cristóbal, Floreana, Santa Cruz, and parts of Isabela have been drastically reduced through predation by introduced rats, cats, dogs, and humans. The doves from Culpepper and Wenman, larger on the average than those from other islands, are considered a distinct race.

It has been suggested that the Galápagos Dove may be closely related to the Zenaida Dove (*Zenaida aurita*) of the West Indies. However, I find the plumage of the Galápagos Dove more similar to that of the Eared Dove (*Zenaida auriculata*) of South America. Obvious similarities between the Galápagos Dove and the Eared Dove are the parallel patches of dark feathers behind the eyes; the size, color, and location of the iridescent green and pink neck patches; and the short tail. The birds differ principally only in size of bill (the Galápagos Dove's is larger) and the amount of white in the wings (the Galápagos Dove has more).

The Eared Dove is widespread on the mainland, including the arid coast of Ecuador, Peru, and Chile. The Galápagos Dove lives mainly in arid habitats, comparable to those in which Eared Doves are likely to be found on the mainland. On Española, Santa Fé, Genovesa, and Rábida, Galápagos Doves are found over the entire island. On large, high islands, they live mainly in the dry lowlands.

The former abundance of Galápagos Doves is reflected in the wealth of fossils I have collected from San Cristóbal, Floreana, Santa Cruz, Rábida, and Isabela (of these islands, doves are common today only on Rábida). Early Galápagos travelers remarked on both the plenitude of doves and their tameness. Many of the birds collected by the California Academy of Sciences Expedition were taken by nooses, hand nets, sticks, and stones. In *The Voyage of the Beagle*, Charles Darwin noted that on Floreana he saw "a boy sitting by a well with a switch in his hand, with which he killed the doves and finches as they came to drink. He had already procured a little heap of them for his dinner; and he said that he had constantly been in the habit of waiting by this well for the same purpose." Galápagos Doves often nest on the ground, and thus their eggs and young are easy targets for introduced predators.

Nonetheless, the doves continue to be extraordinarily tame despite years of human predation. In 1929, A. K. Fisher was reclining in the shade when a Galápagos Dove landed on his knee, walked down to his shoe, and then rested and preened. Through no effort on our part, Galápagos Doves have been regular visitors to our campsites on uninhabited islands. On Santa Fé in 1980, several visited us daily, looking for scraps of rice and oatmeal. One unkempt dove, which was molting heavily and which we called Beatrice, arrived at daybreak every day, watching intently as breakfast was prepared. Beatrice gained quite a bit of weight during our visit.

PLATE 38

Dark-billed Cuckoo   *Coccyzus melacoryphus*

The Dark-billed Cuckoo has only been reported from the Galápagos during the past hundred years. This marks it as a very recent arrival, since the many collectors and other visitors to the islands in earlier years would certainly have reported this readily visible bird had it been present. The species was first recorded in the Galápagos in 1888 from San Cristóbal and Floreana, and in 1901 from Isabela. During 1905–1906, the California Academy of Sciences Expedition recorded the Dark-billed Cuckoo from these same three islands and from Santa Fé, Santa Cruz, and Pinzón, although it was common only on San Cristóbal and Floreana. Today, this cuckoo is firmly established as a resident species on many of the large islands. Such a rapid increase in range and abundance is not unusual for a recent colonizing species. Another example is the Paint-billed Crake, which was first collected in the Galápagos in the 1950s and is now widespread. Specimens of the Galápagos Dark-billed Cuckoo are identical to those from the South American mainland, where it is common in tropical lowlands from Colombia to Argentina. These cuckoos have also colonized two other islands besides the Galápagos—Gorgona and Margarita, off Colombia—and it has even been recorded once in the Falkland Islands.

Fossil studies offer additional evidence that this insect-eating cuckoo has colonized the Galápagos only recently. From the numerous fossil sites I have excavated on San Cristóbal, Floreana, Santa Cruz, Rábida, and Isabela, I have not found a single bone of the Dark-billed Cuckoo. Had this species been present in prehistoric times, its bones would certainly be included among the thousands of fossils that repose in my laboratory. Today, the cuckoo is eaten regularly by Galápagos Barn Owls, so the absence of fossils is not attributable to any unwillingness, on the part of earlier owls, to eat the cuckoos and deposit their bones in the caves.

There is also a behavioral clue to how recently the Dark-billed Cuckoo has colonized the Galápagos: the cuckoos are generally not as tame as the other land birds of the islands. They simply have not been in a predator-free environment long enough to develop the relaxed attitudes so notable in the endemic birds.

In the Galápagos, the Dark-billed Cuckoo prefers to nest in the transition zone or in humid forested areas. Typically it is found in the arid lowlands only outside of the nesting season. But a major change in habitat preference occurred during the El Niño of 1982–83. At that time, cuckoos became extremely common in the "arid" lowlands of many islands, which had been transformed by heavy rains into lush, green jungles. The cuckoo depicted here is one that visited the Charles Darwin Research Station daily in May 1983, feeding on the abundant insect life in sprawling tangles of *Cryptocarpus* bushes. It seems probable that El Niño's of the past century were a significant factor in the rapid and wide dispersal of Dark-billed Cuckoos throughout the archipelago.

PLATE 39

Galápagos Barn Owl *Tyto punctatissima*

This small owl is a personal hero of mine. After all, it is thanks to the digestive processes of many generations of Galápagos Barn Owls that the bones of myriads of small animals were deposited in the islands' lava tubes and became fossils. Were it not for barn owls, my fossil collections would consist only of scattered remains of tortoises, land iguanas, or other animals that had fallen into the caves and perished. Indeed, because of its habit of regurgitating bony pellets in caves, the barn owl is cherished by paleontologists around the world.

The particular barn owl that resides in the Galápagos is an endemic species. It lives today on San Cristóbal, Santa Cruz, Santiago, Isabela, and Fernandina, where it finds the ledges and niches of the lava tubes especially inhabitable. The Galápagos Barn Owl is extinct on Floreana because of predation by introduced mammals. For the same reason, it is rare on San Cristóbal and declining on Santa Cruz, Santiago, and Isabela. In 1984, Godfrey Merlen, Lee, and I found a dead barn owl hanging on a fence on San Cristóbal that had been shot by a local farmer. Such senseless killing still occurs on Santa Cruz and southern Isabela as well. On northern Isabela, where no people live, the current scarcity of barn owls probably results from the abundance of feral cats.

The familiar and nearly worldwide Common Barn Owl (*Tyto alba*) is certainly the ancestor of the Galápagos Barn Owl. Indeed, the Common Barn Owl has colonized many islands around the world, including Indonesia, Melanesia, and Western Polynesia in the Pacific; much of the West Indies; and the Cape Verde Islands in the Atlantic.

The Galápagos Barn Owls are so distinct from all others, in their small size and dark color, that I regard them as an endemic species. The owls Lee has painted here, illuminated by a shaft of light in a lava tube on Santa Cruz, include the dark female (left) and the lighter male (right). Although unmistakably a barn owl, the Galápagos species is darker on the head, back, wings, and tail (both sexes), and the female is much darker on the breast and belly. Most of these differences were noted by John Gould in his original description of the Galápagos Barn Owl in 1839, based on a specimen collected on Santiago by Captain FitzRoy of the *Beagle*.

The various species of barn owls are opportunistic feeders. In mainland habitats, barn owls feed primarily on small mammals, especially rodents, which often comprise up to 95 percent of their diet. On islands, where few or no species of rodents exist, barn owls also feed regularly on snakes, lizards, birds, and bats. If you want to learn which kinds of small vertebrates are living (or used to live) on an island, a collection of barn owl pellets can provide a thorough sample of local fauna.

PLATE 40

Short-eared Owl *Asio flammeus*

Short-eared Owls are common throughout the archipelago and are even found on small islets just off the main islands. This owl hunts and feeds by day or by night. Usually it roosts on the ground, at the foot of a bush or large rock. Although the Short-eared Owl will use rocky cavities as short-term roosts, it does not inhabit deep lava tubes like the Galápagos Barn Owl, from which it also differs significantly in appearance, range, and habits.

Short-eared Owls are extremely widespread in Eurasia as well as in the Americas, including the West Indies, Juan Fernandez Islands, Falkland Islands, and the Pacific coast of South America. Many continental populations are migratory, especially along open coastal regions. The endemic race of Short-eared Owl in the Galápagos has, like the Galápagos Barn Owl, evolved from mainland owls that colonized the islands sometime in the past. Galápagos Short-eared Owls are typically smaller, darker, and more heavily streaked than birds from the mainland.

The Short-eared Owl suffers from the same human-caused woes as the Galápagos Barn Owl. Farmers in the Galápagos still shoot Short-eared owls in the erroneous belief that the owls eat chickens. This has caused a major decline in Short-eared Owl populations on islands inhabited by humans. Furthermore, because the owls nest on the ground, their eggs are vulnerable to trampling or predation by cats, dogs, pigs, goats, donkeys, cattle, or people. The vulnerability of these owls is compounded by their tameness. The Short-eared Owl painted here was observed on South Plaza from four feet away; it did not move an inch during the fifteen quiet minutes we observed it.

Galápagos Short-eared Owls eat mainly rodents and small birds. Their hunting activities tend to be more diurnal in areas where Galápagos Hawks are rare or absent. While on Pinzón in 1984, I noticed that the hunting schedule of local Short-eared Owls was synchronized with that of the local Galápagos Hawks. Every evening at dusk, no more than ten minutes after the last hawks had roosted for the night, two Short-eared Owls visited our campsite. After a full evening of hunting, the two owls retreated to their roosts, about ten minutes before the first hawks appeared at daybreak. This pattern of nonoverlapping predation meant that the introduced black rats so common on Pinzón had a daily allowance of twenty predator-free minutes—a lot more than I would wish them.

PLATE 41

Galápagos Vermilion Flycatcher *Pyrocephalus nanus*

These beautiful little birds have been recorded from all of the major Galápagos islands except San Cristóbal (where there is a distinctly separate species of Vermilion Flycatcher) and Genovesa. They are, however, either very rare, extinct, or have never become established as a breeding species on Española, Santa Fé, Baltra, Rábida, Culpepper, and Wenman. The Galápagos Vermilion Flycatcher exists in two races: one is confined to Santa Cruz; the second is found on other islands of the archipelago. Depicted here, left to right, are an adult female, an adult male, and an immature male, perched in a catclaw tree (*Zanthoxylum fagara*) on Santa Cruz.

The Galápagos Vermilion Flycatcher has evolved from the Vermilion Flycatcher (*Pyrocephalus rubinus*), a species commonly found from the southwestern United States through Central America and much of tropical South America, including the arid Pacific coast of Ecuador and Peru. The Galápagos species has been isolated from its mainland counterpart long enough to have developed significant differences: shorter wings and tails, a lighter and duller shade of red in the adult male plumage, and yellow underparts in adult females rather than the creamy pink, streaked underparts of mainland females. The song of the Galápagos Vermilion Flycatcher also differs from that of its mainland relatives.

I have compared skeletons of Galápagos Vermilion Flycatchers with those of mainland birds and found that the wing bones of the Galápagos species are shorter, while the leg bones are longer. Thus the Galápagos Vermilion Flycatcher keeps a heavier body airborne with smaller wings. As flycatchers typically eat insects on the wing, the Galápagos species has probably reached the maximum weight its small wings can carry.

In the islands, the Galápagos Vermilion Flycatcher is most readily observed in the humid highlands and the transition zone, descending to the arid lowlands only in the nonbreeding season. In arid habitats on the mainland, the Vermilion Flycatcher generally nests along the waterways, where aerial insects are common. An enjoyable part of the fieldwork I used to do in Sonora, Mexico, was listening to the daybreak songs of Vermilion Flycatchers along the mesquite-covered floodplains of small perennial streams. These birds were more active than the Galápagos species and had a louder, livelier song.

Like other endemic Galápagos species, the Galápagos Vermilion Flycatcher is very tame. If you are quiet, it is easy to approach within a few feet. (Indeed, in 1929 A. K. Fisher mentioned that one bird tried to land on his gun barrel.) While mapping the localities of caves in the highlands of Santa Cruz in 1978, Miguel Pozo and I were amused by a small group of two Galápagos Vermilion Flycatchers and ten Warbler Finches that followed us and then perched on our hand-held line as we measured the distances between caves.

PLATE 42

San Cristóbal Vermilion Flycatcher *Pyrocephalus dubius*

The San Cristóbal Vermilion Flycatcher, found only on San Cristóbal, differs enough from the Galápagos Vermilion Flycatcher to be regarded as a distinct species. Although this was recognized by John Gould in 1839 and by many subsequent scientists, ornithologists of the past few decades have nevertheless regarded all vermilion flycatchers in the Galápagos as one species. Compared with the Galápagos Vermilion Flycatcher, the major distinctions of the San Cristóbal Vermilion Flycatcher are its smaller overall size; the paler and pinker undersides and lighter brown of the upperparts in adult males; and the lighter, buffier yellow of the underparts and lighter brown of the upperparts in adult females.

The San Cristóbal Vermilion Flycatcher provides another example of the distinctive nature of the San Cristóbal fauna. Tortoises, leaf-toed geckos, lava lizards, and mockingbirds have also evolved different forms on San Cristóbal, as have several races of Darwin's finches.

The San Cristóbal Vermilion Flycatcher does share the short wing bones and long leg bones that distinguish the Galápagos Vermilion Flycatcher from mainland species. Since smaller wings have reduced the flying range of *both* species, however, this similarity also helps explain why there is little if any genetic exchange between them. San Cristóbal is the easternmost island in the archipelago, where the winds and currents generally run from east to west. In consequence, colonization within the Galápagos probably occurs in one direction, east to west, and the San Cristóbal

populations may well send colonizers but not receive them.

Unfortunately, the San Cristóbal Vermilion Flycatcher has become extremely rare in the humid highlands where it normally nests. A probable reason for its scarcity is that the highlands of San Cristóbal have been inhabited by people for 140 years, and much of the original vegetation has been replaced by introduced plant species that do not support the insects these birds eat. Much of this decline has occurred within the last fifty years, for in July and August 1929 A. K. Fisher found these birds all along the main trail that runs from the arid western coast to the village of Progreso in the highlands.

This plate shows a pair of San Cristóbal Vermilion Flycatchers perched on a tortoise (*Geochelone elephantopus chathamensis*). I must confess that I have never seen them together on this island, where both species have become rare, but I have seen Galápagos Vermilion Flycatchers perched on tortoises on Santa Cruz. Maybe I enjoy this painting because it depicts a situation that must have been common on many of the islands—including San Cristóbal—prior to human settlement, when flycatchers wandered to the lowlands during the nonbreeding season. In any event, this plate is a striking portrayal of the interspecies harmony of vertebrate life in the Galápagos—the flycatcher perches gingerly on the relatively motionless tortoise, neither realizing they last shared a common ancestor some 300 million years ago, well before the Age of Dinosaurs.

PLATE 43

Large-billed Flycatcher *Myiarchus magnirostris*

The Large-billed Flycatcher is an endemic species that is widespread in the Galápagos. The bird has had other names—Papa Moscas, María, Galápagos Flycatcher, Yellow-bellied Flycatcher, Galápagos Tyrant Flycatcher, and Broad-billed Flycatcher—but the one that has stuck is Large-billed Flycatcher. This is a bit odd considering that this species has one of the *smallest* bills of any of the *Myiarchus* flycatchers.

Large-billed Flycatchers are common today on most of the islands. They are rare or absent, however, on certain small, dry islands such as Española, Santa Fé, Rábida, and Wenman. In spite of its wide distribution, the Large-billed Flycatcher varies remarkably little from island to island. This suggests that the birds either move regularly among the islands or their evolution as a distinct species has occurred relatively recently.

The mainland species of *Myiarchus* flycatcher that seems the most likely ancestor of the Large-billed Flycatcher is the Dusky-capped Flycatcher (*Myiarchus tuberculifer*). It closely resembles the Galápagos species in plumage characteristics and —ironically—is the only other species of *Myiarchus* flycatcher that has a bill as *small* as the "Large-billed" Flycatcher. The Dusky-capped Flycatcher is widespread in the Americas, occurring from the southwestern United States to Argentina, and is closely related to two other insular flycatchers besides the Large-billed Flycatcher. (One of these lives on the Tres Marías Islands off the Pacific coast of Mexico; the other is found only in Jamaica. Interestingly, characters by which these two insular flycatchers differ from their mainland relatives are similar to those found in the Galápagos Large-billed Flycatchers.)

The Large-billed Flycatcher quickly becomes familiar to every visitor to the Galápagos. It nests at all elevations, wherever it can find cavities in trees or cacti. Where natural cavities are scarce, Large-billed Flycatchers have even been known to take over the abandoned nests of Darwin's finches.

It would be difficult to overestimate the tameness of the Large-billed Flycatcher. Rollo Beck, the most productive and enthusiastic collector ever to visit the Galápagos, noted that most specimens of Large-billed Flycatcher taken in 1905–1906 were procured not by shooting but by hitting the birds with gun barrels.

My own most memorable experience with this flycatcher was in August 1978 on Santa Cruz, in the thorny forest just north of Academy Bay. The bird was perched at eye level, about 2 meters away, when I decided to photograph it. While I was looking at it through the lens, the flycatcher left its perch and flew directly onto my head. It snapped at something in my hair for several seconds and returned to its post.

Once again I tried to focus my camera, but the bird soon made an identical flight to my head, snapped at something, and flew back to its perch. Now totally entertained by our amusing relationship, I tried once more to photograph friend *Myiarchus*. Before I could trip the shutter, it flew again to my head for a few more seconds of frantic bill-snapping. Then, returning satisfied to the perch, the flycatcher graciously posed for several photographs before flying away to new adventures. Having been in the field for quite some time, I questioned whether my hair, which had not known comb for days, was free of edible ectoparasites. Since Large-billed Flycatchers do line their nests with hair and feathers, I reasoned the bird was simply robbing my scalp to dress its nest. Still I found myself scratching my head suspiciously and soon retreated to the Darwin Station for a badly needed shower.

Later I learned that my experience was not unique, for others have reported Large-billed Flycatchers landing on their heads for choice nest material. The next time you see a Large-billed Flycatcher, stand very still and you too may have a chance to contribute to its home.

PLATE 44

Southern Martin   *Progne concolor*

Like all members of the swallow family, the Southern Martin uses its remarkable aerial skills to catch insects on the wing. Here Lee has depicted a typical pair—a glossy purple male and a grayish brown female. The Southern Martin is one of the mystery birds of the Galápagos: little is known about its evolution or habits, and neither the size of the island population of martins nor its distribution has been studied. It has been recorded from all of the main islands except Genovesa, Marchena, Pinta, Wenman, and Culpepper, but the Southern Martin lives in small, isolated groups and is not common anywhere.

In Bolivia, Paraguay, Uruguay, and Argentina, Southern Martins are not uncommon. These continental birds are larger than those in the islands, but a race of Southern Martins lives along the arid coast of Peru and northern Chile that is so similar in size and coloration to the Galápagos Southern Martins that both are thought to be the same race. The Galápagos bird tends to be a bit smaller than its mainland relative, but this difference is not great enough to justify considering the Galápagos Southern Martin an endemic race.

We do know that Southern Martins, both in the Galápagos and along the coast of Peru, usually roost and nest in natural cavities and crevices in cliffs, often near the sea, and thus appear fairly safe from the predators that threaten many species. It is hoped that ornithologists will one day turn their attention to this attractive, but relatively unspectacular species, and help us to understand how and when these birds came to the Galápagos, and how they adapted to their island habitat.

PLATE 45

Galápagos Mockingbird   *Mimus parvulus*

San Cristóbal Mockingbird   *Mimus melanotis*

The four endemic species of mockingbirds in the Galápagos can be divided into two major groups. The first includes the San Cristóbal Mockingbird (lower bird) and the more widespread Galápagos Mockingbird (two upper birds). These two species are smaller and have grayer upperparts, whiter underparts, and a shorter bill than the species of the second group, consisting of the Española Mockingbird and the Floreana Mockingbird (see plate 46).

The San Cristóbal Mockingbird is found only on San Cristóbal, whereas the Galápagos Mockingbird is found on all major islands except San Cristóbal, Española, Floreana, and Pinzón. The various populations of Galápagos Mockingbird are further divided into four to seven subspecies characterized mainly by differences in length of the wing, tail, bill, and feet.

The mockingbirds in the Galápagos evolved from a colonization of the archipelago by an ancestral population of the Long-tailed Mockingbird (*Mimus longicaudatus*), a common species along the arid Pacific coast of Ecuador and Peru. Both species are streaked on the head and back and are less pure gray above; they also share a similar facial pattern, long bills and feet, and similar nesting habits. The San Cristóbal and Galápagos Mockingbirds are more similar to the Long-tailed Mockingbird, in plumage and in size proportions, than are the Española or Floreana Mockingbirds. The closeness of this relationship is emphasized by the fact that the Galápagos Mockingbird has successfully mated with the Long-tailed Mockingbird in captivity but not with either the Española Mockingbird or the Floreana Mockingbird.

San Cristóbal was probably the first island colonized by the Long-tailed Mockingbird. After residing on this island for an unknown period of time, during which some evolution undoubtedly took place, two major dispersals occurred. The first was to the west and northwest to most of the other major islands, and members of this group evolved into the Galápagos Mockingbird. The second dispersal was to the southwest, and from these birds came the Española and Floreana Mockingbirds. Relatively little additional evolutionary change occurred in the first group, whereas the second group has diverged significantly from the mainland species as well as from the other species in the Galápagos.

As is true also for the endemic Galápagos species of vermilion flycatchers and Darwin's finches, the species of mockingbirds in the Galápagos have evolved shorter wings and tails than their mainland ancestors. This, combined with behavioral changes, has resulted in the reduced ability of mockingbirds to spread beyond their present range in the islands today. For example, the Galápagos Mockingbird became extinct on Baltra in the 1940s. Yet during the past forty years, mockingbirds from Santa Cruz have not, as far as I know, even crossed the narrow channel (less than half a mile wide) that separates Santa Cruz from Baltra.

A major mockingbird mystery is why none is found on Pinzón, an island surrounded by other islands where Galápagos Mockingbirds thrive. (On only two occasions over the past eighty years has a single stray mockingbird been sighted on Pinzón.) In terms of size and elevation Pinzón provides habitat suitable for mockingbirds, yet none of these birds resides there. It has been suggested that Pinzón's lack of palo santo trees (*Bursera graveolens*) might provide an explanation. But while mockingirds on other islands do eat palo santo seeds and occasionally nest in palo santo trees, they are by no means dependent on them. I had hoped to uncover fossils of mockingbirds on Pinzón in 1984, but unfortunately I found no lava tubes on this island. I did see (and feel) a great predominance of mesquite (*Prosopis juliflora*) and catclaw (*Zanthoxylum fagara*), but neither of these thorny trees seems to attract mockingbirds elsewhere in the Galápagos. It may be that the low level of overall botanical diversity on Pinzón, rather than the simple lack of palo santo trees, explains the birds' mysterious absence.

PLATE 46

Española Mockingbird   *Mimus macdonaldi*

Floreana Mockingbird   *Mimus trifasciatus*

These two mockingbirds are more closely related to each other than to the species described in the previous plate. To generalize, they are larger, browner, and have longer bills; they also differ significantly in their behavior, spending more time on the ground than the other two species. The Española Mockingbird is found only on Española and the small island of Gardner-near-Española. The Floreana Mockingbird, perched here on a prickly pear cactus, no longer lives on Floreana but can be found on Floreana's satellite islands of Champion and Gardner-near-Floreana.

The Española Mockingbird, which has the longest bill of all mockingbirds in the Galápagos, is very much of a scavenger and has acquired a reputation for breaking and eating seabird eggs. It watches the ground and brushy vegetation of Española with an alert eye, feeding on practically anything edible from seeds and flowers to lava lizards, insects, spiders, bird eggs, and sea lion afterbirth. The Española Mockingbird is also tamer and more inquisitive than other mockingbirds. Many tourists on Española have had these mockingbirds perch curiously on their heads or shoulders, or even on their cameras.

The Floreana Mockingbird is also an omnivorous feeder that spends considerable time on the ground, often near the shore. However, the Floreana Mockingbird is unique in that it nests exclusively in prickly pear cactus, where it also does much of its feeding. During three days on Champion Island, all of the mockingbirds that I saw were either in prickly pears or on the ground. Interestingly, this habit may explain why this mockingbird has vanished from the island that gave it its name.

Captain David Porter of the U.S. frigate *Essex* first noted mockingbirds on Floreana in 1813, and specimens were collected by Charles Darwin and Captain FitzRoy in 1835. After the *Beagle* expedition, occasional reports were made and one more specimen collected, but by the 1870s mockingbirds no longer existed on Floreana. All major expeditions of the past hundred years have failed to find them, although the birds continue to survive on the small, offshore islands of Champion and Gardner-near-Floreana.

Some ornithologists began to doubt that the Floreana Mockingbird ever occurred on the island for which it was named. Recent evidence has shown, however, that the mockingbird did indeed live on Floreana. The first was archival research by biohistorian Frank Sulloway, who, in carefully documenting the localities of *Beagle* specimens of Darwin's finches, also straightened out a controversy about the accuracy of certain labels of other *Beagle* specimens. The second was my own fossil research. In 1978 and 1980, I discovered 446 fossil bones of Floreana Mockingbirds in 4 different lava tubes on northern Floreana. These bones were from several hundred to several thousand years old.

So why did the Floreana Mockingbird become extinct on Floreana? The answer seems simple when you look at the human history of the island. Floreana was colonized by several hundred people in 1832, just three years before the *Beagle*'s visit, and with them they brought rats, cats, dogs, pigs, goats, cattle, donkeys, and horses. Seeking food and fresh water, these animals soon depleted the prickly pear cactus in the lowlands of the island. The Floreana Mockingbird saw its homes eaten away by the introduced herbivores. Fortunately, these unwelcome newcomers have not colonized Champion and Gardner-near-Floreana, where the vegetation remains in pristine condition.

PLATE 47

Yellow Warbler   *Dendroica petechia*

Bright, cheery, vocal, and aggressive, the Yellow Warbler is impossible to overlook on nearly any sizable island in the Galápagos. One of the most common and abundant land birds, it is found in brushy or forested habitats throughout the islands, regardless of elevation. Along the coast, Yellow Warblers are especially prevalent in mangroves or, as shown here, in manzanillo trees (*Hippomane mancinella*).

The Yellow Warbler is an extremely widespread species in the Americas, ranging from Alaska and Labrador to the West Indies and coastal South America. Within this range, the Yellow Warbler has many distinct races, particularly in the West Indies and along the coast of Central and northern South America. Many of the tropical forms live only along the coast, where they are especially fond of mangrove stands.

The race of Yellow Warbler found in the Galápagos also occurs on Cocos Island, between the Galápagos and Central America. This race differs from most other tropical forms of Yellow Warbler but closely resembles a mainland variety that lives on the Pacific coast of Colombia, Ecuador, and northern Peru. Males of the mainland race are a slightly brighter shade of yellow—their breasts and bellies are slightly more streaked—than the birds from the Galápagos and Cocos islands.

The Yellow Warblers depicted here include an adult male (upper center), an adult female (right center), and two immatures (below). Those familiar with North American Yellow Warblers will notice that the Galápagos birds have highly distinct plumages, especially the female and immature.

In spite of the fact that Galápagos Barn Owls regularly eat Yellow Warblers today, I have never found a fossil of this bird in the Galápagos. As in the case of the Dark-billed Cuckoo, this suggests that the Yellow Warbler is a relatively recent colonizer of the archipelago. Because Yellow Warblers were noted in the Galápagos as early as 1835 and are also slightly different from the mainland birds, I believe they colonized the Galápagos somewhat earlier than Dark-billed Cuckoos.

Yellow Warblers everywhere are rather bold. Typically, if you make some sort of "pishing" or squeaking sound, they respond rapidly and aggressively, allowing you to see them at close range. This is true in the apple orchards of our farm in Pennsylvania, where I first became acquainted with the Yellow Warbler. Not surprisingly, the drama is even greater in the Galápagos, where territorial males fly frantically from perch to perch and hover within a few feet of anyone who intrudes on their turf.

PLATE 48

Sharp-beaked Ground Finch   *Geospiza nebulosa*

Small Ground Finch   *Geospiza fuliginosa*

Medium Ground Finch   *Geospiza fortis*

Large Ground Finch   *Geospiza magnirostris*

The four species of "ground finches" are among the best studied of any Darwin's finches. The anatomical differences that distinguish these species of ground finches from each other are overall body size and, most importantly, the size and shape of their bills. The plumages are nearly identical; adult males are black and adult females are streaked brown. In this plate, a male Sharp-beaked Ground Finch is flying above a male Small Ground Finch (left) and a female Medium Ground Finch (right). At the bottom are a female Large Ground Finch (left), of the race that still survives, and a male Large Ground Finch (right), of the race that once inhabited San Cristóbal and Floreana. As in all species of Darwin's finches, the color of the bill indicates the bird's breeding status. Those with pure black bills are in breeding condition, whereas those with yellowish bills, as depicted in this plate, are not.

Small, Medium, and Large Ground Finches are usually found in the arid lowlands, where they forage on the ground or in low vegetation. The Small Ground Finch lives on all major islands except Genovesa, Culpepper, and perhaps Wenman; those from Marchena and Pinta are smaller than the rest. The Medium Ground Finch occurs on all major islands except Genovesa and Culpepper, although it is very rare or may even be extinct on Española and Wenman. No distinct races are recognized for the Medium Ground Finch. The Large Ground Finch lives, or used to live, on all major islands except Española and Culpepper; often it is less common than the other ground finches. A huge variety of Large Ground Finch, now extinct, inhabited San Cristóbal and Floreana. Finally the Sharp-beaked Ground Finch occurs, or did until recently, mainly in the humid highlands on San Cristóbal, Floreana, Santa Cruz, Santiago, Isabela, Fernandina, and Pinta. However, on the small, low islands of Genovesa, Culpepper, and Wenman it lives, by necessity, in arid habitats. The Sharp-beaked Ground Finch is extinct on San Cristóbal, Floreana, and Santa Cruz, and its status on Isabela and Fernandina is poorly known.

The Large Ground Finch became extinct on San Cristóbal and Floreana for much the same reason as the Floreana Mockingbird—destruction of prickly pear cactus in the lowlands by feral herbivores, particularly goats and donkeys. Fossils from Floreana show that in prehistoric times, the Large Ground Finch was very abundant. The reason for the extinction of Sharp-beaked Ground Finches on San Cristóbal, Floreana, and Santa Cruz is less clear but is probably related to changes in highland habitats that occurred soon after human settlement.

The distinctions among the Small, Medium, and Large Ground Finches are poorly defined. The Medium Ground Finch, in particular, is difficult to identify with any assurance. On Floreana or Santa Cruz, for example, a small individual of the Medium Ground Finch may be identical to a large individual of the Small Ground Finch, whereas a large individual of the Medium Ground Finch may be just like a small individual of the Large Ground Finch. If all this sounds confusing, it helps to know that ornithologists are confused too. I believe many ground finches cannot be pigeonholed into one species or the other.

The ground finches are crucial to evolutionary studies, because they (particularly the Sharp-beaked Ground Finch and the Small Ground Finch) are the most similar to the ancestral form of Darwin's finch, and therefore represent the important first step in the truly extraordinary evolutionary succession that has resulted in today's assortment of Galápagos finches. As discussed in the text, I believe the living Blue-black Grassquit (*Geospiza jacarina*) is the ancestor of all Darwin's finches. There are striking resemblances in the plumages and skulls between the grassquit and Darwin's finches. Blue-black Grassquits are widespread in tropical lowlands from Mexico through much of South America, including the Pacific coast of South America from Colombia to northern Chile. The origin of Darwin's finches, in such a view, is not unusual or inexplicable. It was all started by the common and conspicuous little grassquit, to which many ornithologists, myself included, owe a great debt.

PLATE 49

Small Cactus Finch *Geospiza scandens*

Large Cactus Finch *Geospiza conirostris*

Vegetarian Finch *Geospiza crassirostris*

Although they spend much of their time in trees or cacti, these three species probably evolved directly from the "ground finch" group of Darwin's finches. In this plate, Lee has depicted female and male Vegetarian Finches in the upper left and upper right. Just below the male Vegetarian Finch is a male Large Cactus Finch. Along the bottom are a male and a female Small Cactus Finch. Note that all of these birds have black bills, indicating they are in breeding condition.

The Small Cactus Finch occurs on all major islands except Española, Fernandina, Genovesa, Culpepper, and Wenman. Several different races can be recognized by experts. Its absence from Fernandina is strange, for the island has plenty of suitable habitat. Likewise, the scarcity of Small Cactus Finches on Pinzón, where prickly pear cactus is common, is difficult to explain.

The Large Cactus Finch is found only on Española, Genovesa, Culpepper, and Wenman. The race on Española has a thicker bill than birds from Genovesa, Culpepper, and Wenman. The Large Cactus Finch spends a greater percentage of its time on the ground than the Small Cactus Finch.

The Vegetarian Finch lives mainly on islands with humid highlands, namely, San Cristóbal, Floreana, Santa Cruz, Isabela, Fernandina, and Pinta. It has been recorded as well from Pinzón, Rábida, and Marchena, but I am not sure of its current status on these three rather small, dry islands. The Vegetarian Finch varies remarkably little from island to island; no distinct races are recognized.

The Vegetarian Finch has been regarded as a very distinctive species that is nonetheless closely related to the "tree finches" depicted in the next plate. I believe, however, that the Vegetarian Finch is more closely related to the ground finches than to the tree finches. The male plumage of Vegetarian Finches is similar to that of ground finches (although the female plumage does resemble that of tree finches). Numerous fossil bills that I have collected on Santa Cruz are intermediate in size and shape between the Vegetarian Finch and the Medium Ground Finch. Right now I am uncertain whether these fossil specimens should be classified as a Vegetarian Finch, a Medium Ground Finch, or an unknown species. They may represent hybrids between the two species. Regardless, the fossils suggest that the Vegetarian Finch is not very distinct from the ground finches.

In sites from the lowlands of both Santa Cruz and Floreana, I have found quite a few fossils of true Vegetarian Finches. In fact they are more common than I expected, based on the bird's current scarcity in lowland habitats, where they are typically found only outside of the nesting season. There are no detailed studies of the feeding habits of the Vegetarian Finch, but it is presumed to eat mainly fruits, soft seeds, and some insects. Further studies may help explain the bird's current distribution and why it is less common now than it apparently used to be.

PLATE 50

Small Tree Finch   *Geospiza parvula*

Medium Tree Finch   *Geospiza pauper*

Large Tree Finch   *Geospiza psittacula*

The "tree finch" group of Darwin's finches includes these three species, which are closely related to those depicted in the following plate as well. All tree finches are arboreal and largely insectivorous. They breed mainly in the transition zone or higher up, often descending into the arid lowlands outside of the nesting season. Tree finches have paler plumages than the ground finches, cactus finches, or Vegetarian Finches. The plumages of the Small, Medium, and Large Tree Finch are essentially identical; these species are distinguished from one another by differences in overall size and in the sizes of their similarly shaped bills. This plate shows, from left to right, a female and male Large Tree Finch, a male Medium Tree Finch, and a female and male Small Tree Finch. As in the other three plates of Darwin's finches, such a gathering would be practically impossible to observe in the wild, but is pictured here so that the species can be easily compared.

The Small Tree Finch lives on all of the major islands except Española, Genovesa, Marchena, and Culpepper, with the birds from San Cristóbal being distinctly smaller than the rest. The Large Tree Finch, of which several races exist, is found on all major islands except Española, Genovesa, Culpepper, and Wenman, although it is either rare, extinct, or was never established on Santa Fé, Baltra, Pinzón, and

Rábida. The Large Tree Finch has been reported to be rare on San Cristóbal, but during a visit there in 1984 we saw them fairly commonly on the humid, forested slopes of windward southern San Cristóbal. I should say that the birds we saw *seemed* to be typical Large Tree Finches. I have a hard time believing even my own sight records of Darwin's finches.

The fact that the Medium Tree Finch is confined to Floreana is puzzling. As its name suggests, this species is midway in size between Small and Large Tree Finches. Why should Floreana be the only island inhabited by three different tree finches? One answer is that there may not actually be three distinct species: the Medium Tree Finch may simply be a hybrid between the Small and Large Tree Finches. The measurements of Medium Tree Finches overlap with those of Small Tree Finches and Large Tree Finches from Floreana. Small Tree Finches are common on the island, but Large Tree Finches are rare. Perhaps a scarcity of mates once encouraged certain Large Tree Finches to mate with the much more common Small Tree Finches. Eventually, this may have nearly eliminated the Large Tree Finches, leaving a new hybrid population with characteristics of both parent groups.

PLATE 51

Woodpecker Finch *Geospiza pallida*

Mangrove Finch *Geospiza heliobates*

Warbler Finch *Geospiza olivacea*

The Woodpecker, Mangrove, and Warbler Finches are mainly insectivorous birds that live in trees. An important difference distinguishing these three species from all other Darwin's finches is that their male and female plumages are alike. The pale plumages of the Woodpecker, Mangrove, and Warbler Finches are, however, very similar to those of female tree finches. Another important feature in these three species is that, in keeping with their insectivorous diets, the bills of all three have become slimmer than those of their seed-eating relatives—a distinction that reaches its most extreme form in the appropriately named Warbler Finch. In this plate we see three different races of the Warbler Finch (top two birds, and lower left). A Mangrove Finch is perched in the center, and a Woodpecker Finch below, holding a small twig in its bill.

The Woodpecker Finch is the best known of all Darwin's finches because of its habit of using twigs or cactus spines to pry insect larvae out of small holes or from under tree bark. It nests in the humid highlands of San Cristóbal, Santa Cruz, Pinzón, Santiago, Isabela, and Fernandina, and is represented by several races. On Floreana, Rábida, Santa Fé, and Pinta, the Woodpecker Finch is either very rare, extinct, or was never established as a breeding species.

The Mangrove Finch occurs only in isolated stretches of wooded coastline on Isabela and Fernandina. This poorly studied species is extremely similar in appearance to the Woodpecker Finch. It is also very rare today and may be threatened by the world's rising sea level, which is eroding mangrove forests where the bird habitually resides.

The Warbler Finch is the only species of Darwin's finch that is found on all major islands. On large islands with humid highlands, it usually nests in the highlands, but outside of the nesting season can be found anywhere. It also thrives on small islands that have only arid habitats. I recognize nine different races of the Warbler Finch, characterized mostly by differences in bill size and plumage coloration.

The Warbler Finch is the smallest of Darwin's finches, and is distinctive above all because it has evolved a thin, warblerlike bill, adapted for insect-eating. It was John Gould who first noted in his descriptions of the *Beagle* specimens—to Darwin's great surprise—that this small bird is a finch rather than a warbler.

For many years, Gould's identification was questioned by ornithologists who insisted that the Warbler Finch was a warbler, or perhaps a honeycreeper, but certainly not a finch. Since the turn of the century, however, studies of both anatomy and behavior have clearly demonstrated Gould was right.

In spite of its small bill, the Warbler Finch is anatomically similar to other Galápagos finches. Even more conclusively, the Warbler Finch hybridizes occasionally with the Small Tree Finch or the Woodpecker Finch on many islands, where these three species live side-by-side in the humid highlands. (Their nesting habits are practically identical.) If the Warbler Finch were not a true finch, or if it were even truly aberrant among Darwin's finches, such hybridization would not occur.

It is worth noting that one species of "Darwin's" finch lives outside of the Galápagos. This is the Cocos Finch (*Geospiza inornata*), confined to Cocos Island, several hundred miles northeast of the Galápagos. Because of its rather narrow, elongated bill, it has been suggested that the Cocos Finch is more closely related to the Warbler Finch than to any other Darwin's finches. However, the bill of the Cocos Finch, which is adapted for obtaining a variety of insects, nectar, and small seeds, is quite unlike that of any other species of Darwin's finch, including the Warbler Finch. I believe the Cocos Finch evolved from an independent colonization of Cocos Island by our friend the Blue-black Grassquit, which is nearly identical in plumage.

English and Spanish Names of the Galápagos Islands

Italicized names are those most commonly used in the Galápagos today.
(Modified from Slevin, 1959:25–26.)

English Names	Spanish Names
Abingdon	*Pinta*, Geraldino
Albany	
Albemarle	*Isabela*, Santa Gertrudis
Barrington	*Sante Fé*
Bartholomew	*Bartolomé*
Beagle	
Bindloe	*Marchena*, Torres
Brattle	*Tortuga*
Caldwell	
Champion	
Charles	*Floreana*, Santa María
Chatham, Dassigney	*San Cristóbal*, Grande
Cowley	
Crossman	*Los Hermanos*
Culpepper, Darwin	Guerra
Daphne Major	
Daphne Minor	
Duncan, Dean	*Pinzón*
Eden	
Enderby	
Gardner-near-Charles	*Gardner-near-Floreana*
Gardner-near-Hood	*Gardner-near-Española*
Guy Fawkes	
Hood	*Española*
Indefatigable, Norfolk, Porter	*Santa Cruz*, Bolivia, Valdez, Chavez, San Clemente
James, York	*Santiago*, San Salvador, Gil, Olmedo
Jensen	*Caamaño*
Jervis	*Rábida*
Nameless, Bewel Rock	*Sin Nombre*
Narborough	*Fernandina*, Plata
North Plaza	*Plaza Norte*
North Seymour	*Seymour Norte*, Seymour
Onslow	
South Plaza	*Plaza Sur*
South Seymour	*Baltra*
Tower, Ewres	*Genovesa*
Watson	
Wenman, Wolf	Nuñez, Gasna, Genovesa Ewres

Resident Species of the Galápagos

For reptiles and mammals, the range of each species is given. The ranges of birds are discussed in the plate captions as they are usually more complex and difficult to summarize in list form.

Reptiles

- *Geochelone elephantopus*—Galápagos Tortoise
  All major islands except Genovesa, Marchena, Culpepper, Wenman; extinct on
  Floreana, Santa Fé, Rábida, and perhaps Fernandina
  Chelonia mydas agassizii—Green Turtle
  Widespread marine species
  Phyllodactylus tuberculosus—Tuberculated Leaf-toed Gecko
  San Cristóbal
- *Phyllodactylus gilberti*—Wenman Leaf-toed Gecko
  Wenman
- *Phyllodactylus leei*—San Cristóbal Leaf-toed Gecko
  San Cristóbal
- *Phyllodactylus barringtonensis*—Santa Fé Leaf-toed Gecko
  Santa Fé
- *Phyllodactylus galapagoensis*—Galápagos Leaf-toed Gecko
  Santa Cruz, Daphne Major, Santiago, Pinzón, Cowley, Tortuga, Isabela, Fernandina
- *Phyllodactylus,* species undetermined—Rábida Leaf-toed Gecko
  Rábida (E?)
- *Phyllodactylus bauri*—Baur's Leaf-toed Gecko
  Española, Gardner-near-Española, Floreana, Gardner-near-Floreana, Enderby, Champion
- *Tropidurus pacificus*—Pinta Lava Lizard
  Pinta
- *Tropidurus duncanensis*—Pinzón Lava Lizard
  Pinzón
- *Tropidurus habelii*—Marchena Lava Lizard
  Marchena
- *Tropidurus bivittatus*—San Cristóbal Lava Lizard
  San Cristóbal
- *Tropidurus delanonis*—Española Lava Lizard
  Española, Gardner-near-Española
- *Tropidurus grayii*—Floreana Lava Lizard
  Floreana, Gardner-near-Floreana, Caldwell, Enderby, Champion
- *Tropidurus albemarlensis*—Galápagos Lava Lizard
  Santa Fé, Santa Cruz, Santiago, Rábida, Isabela, Fernandina
- *Conolophus subcristatus*—Land Iguana
  Santa Cruz, Baltra, Seymour Norte, Santiago, Rábida, Isabela, Fernandina
- *Conolophus pallidus*—Santa Fé Land Iguana
  Santa Fé
- *Amblyrhynchus cristatus*—Marine Iguana
  All major islands
- *Alsophis biserialis biserialis*—Floreana Snake
  Floreana, Gardner-near-Floreana, Champion

- *Alsophis biserialis eibli*—San Cristóbal Snake
  San Cristóbal
- *Alsophis biserialis hoodensis*—Española Snake
  Española, Gardner-near-Española
- *Alsophis dorsalis dorsalis*—Galápagos Snake
  Santa Fé, Santa Cruz, Baltra, Santiago, Rábida
- *Alsophis dorsalis helleri*—Isabela Snake
  Isabela, Tortuga
- *Alsophis dorsalis occidentalis*—Fernandina Snake
  Fernandina
- *Alsophis slevini slevini*—Slevin's Snake
  Pinzón, Isabela, Fernandina
- *Alsophis slevini steindachneri*—Steindachner's Snake
  Santa Cruz, Baltra, Santiago, Rábida
  Pelamis platurus—Yellow-bellied Sea Snake
  Widespread marine species

Mammals

- *Lasiurus borealis brachyotis*—Red Bat
  San Cristóbal, Floreana, Santa Cruz
  Lasiurus cinereus—Hoary Bat
  Santa Cruz
- *Arctocephalus galapagoensis*—Galápagos Fur Seal
  Nearly throughout the archipelago
- *Zalophus californianus wollebaeki*—California Sea Lion
  Throughout the archipelago
- *Oryzomys galapagoensis*—San Cristóbal Rice Rat
  San Cristóbal
- *Oryzomys bauri*—Santa Fé Rice Rat
  Santa Fé
- *Nesoryzomys indefessus*—Large Santa Cruz Rice Rat
  Santa Cruz, Baltra
- *Nesoryzomys swarthi*—Large Santiago Rice Rat
  Santiago
- *Nesoryzomys,* undescribed species—Large Rábida Rice Rat
  Rábida
- *Nesoryzomys,* undescribed species—Large Isabela Rice Rat
  Isabela
- *Nesoryzomys narboroughi*—Large Fernandina Rice Rat
  Fernandina
- *Nesoryzomys darwini*—Small Santa Cruz Rice Rat
  Santa Cruz
- *Nesoryzomys,* undescribed species—Small Isabela Rice Rat
  Isabela
- *Nesoryzomys fernandinae*—Small Fernandina Rice Rat
  Fernandina
- *Megaoryzomys curioi*—Santa Cruz Giant Rat
  Santa Cruz
- *Megaoryzomys,* undescribed species—Isabela Giant Rat
  Isabela

Marine Birds

- *Spheniscus mendiculus*—Galápagos Penguin
  Diomedea leptorhyncha—Waved Albatross
  [Nearly endemic, but breeds in small numbers on Isla La Plata, off Ecuador.]
- *Pterodroma phaeopygia phaeopygia*—Dark-rumped Petrel
- *Puffinus lherminieri subalaris*—Audubon's Shearwater
- *Oceanites gracilis galapagoensis*—White-vented Storm-Petrel
- *Oceanodroma tethys tethys*—Wedge-rumped Storm-Petrel

Oceanodroma castro—Band-rumped Storm-Petrel
Phaethon aethereus mesonauta—Red-billed Tropicbird
- *Pelecanus occidentalis urinator*—Brown Pelican
- *Sula nebouxii excisa*—Blue-footed Booby
Sula dactylatra granti—Masked Booby
Sula sula websteri—Red-footed Booby
- *Phalacrocorax harrisi*—Flightless Cormorant
Fregata minor ridgwayi—Great Frigatebird
Fregata magnificens—Magnificent Frigatebird
- *Haematopus palliatus galapagensis*—American Oystercatcher
- *Larus fuliginosus*—Lava Gull
Larus furcatus—Swallow-tailed Gull
[Nearly endemic, but breeds on Isla Malpelo, off Colombia.]
Sterna fuscata crissalis—Sooty Tern
- *Anous stolidus galapagensis*—Brown Noddy

Aquatic Birds

- *Ardea herodias cognata*—Great Blue Heron
Ardea alba egretta—Great Egret
- *Ardeola sundevalli*—Lava Heron
Ardeola striata cf. *striata*—Striated Heron
- *Nyctanassa violacea pauper*—Yellow-crowned Night-Heron
- *Laterallus jamaicensis spilonotus*—Black Rail
Neocrex erythrops—Paint-billed Crake
Gallinula chloropus [*cachinnans* or *pauxilla*]—Common Gallinule
Himantopus himantopus mexicanus—Common Stilt
- *Phoenicopterus ruber glyphorhynchus*—Greater Flamingo
- *Anas bahamensis galapagensis*—White-cheeked Pintail

Land Birds

- *Buteo galapagoensis*—Galápagos Hawk
- *Zenaida galapagoensis*—Galápagos Dove
Coccyzus melacoryphus—Dark-billed Cuckoo
- *Tyto punctatissima*—Galápagos Barn Owl
- *Asio flammeus galapagoensis*—Short-eared Owl
- *Pyrocephalus nanus*—Galápagos Vermilion Flycatcher
- *Pyrocephalus dubius*—San Cristóbal Vermilion Flycatcher
- *Myiarchus magnirostris*—Large-billed Flycatcher
Progne concolor—Southern Martin
- *Mimus parvulus*—Galápagos Mockingbird
- *Mimus melanotis*—San Cristóbal Mockingbird
- *Mimus macdonaldi*—Española Mockingbird
- *Mimus trifasciatus*—Floreana Mockingbird
Dendroica petechia aureola—Yellow Warbler
- *Geospiza nebulosa*—Sharp-beaked Ground Finch
- *Geospiza fuliginosa*—Small Ground Finch
- *Geospiza fortis*—Medium Ground Finch
- *Geospiza magnirostris*—Large Ground Finch
- *Geospiza scandens*—Small Cactus Finch
- *Geospiza conirostris*—Large Cactus Finch
- *Geospiza crassirostris*—Vegetarian Finch
- *Geospiza parvula*—Small Tree Finch
- *Geospiza pauper*—Medium Tree Finch
- *Geospiza psittacula*—Large Tree Finch
- *Geospiza pallida*—Woodpecker Finch
- *Geospiza heliobates*—Mangrove Finch
- *Geospiza olivacea*—Warbler Finch

Select Bibliography

The titles listed here are not comprehensive. They are meant to introduce the reader to a variety of popular and scientific literature on the natural history of the Galápagos and related topics. Titles preceded by an asterisk (*) are primarily scientific in nature, although many also contain general information about the islands and their wildlife.

Beebe, William. 1924. *Galápagos: World's End.* New York: G. P. Putnam's Sons.

*Bell, Thomas. 1843. *Reptiles.* Part 5 of *The Zoology of the Voyage of H. M. S. Beagle, under the Command of Captain Robert FitzRoy, R. N., during the Years 1832 to 1836,* edited by Charles Darwin. London: Smith, Elder and Co.

*Berry, R. J., editor. 1985. Evolution in the Galápagos Islands. *Biological Journal of the Linnean Society* 21:1–270.

Black, Juan. 1973. *Galápagos, Archipielago del Ecuador.* Quito, Ecuador: Imprenta Europa.

*Bowman, Robert I., editor. 1966. *The Galápagos: Proceedings of the Galápagos International Scientific Project.* Berkeley: University of California Press.

*———, Margaret Berson, and Alan E. Leviton, editors. 1983. *Patterns of Evolution in Galápagos Organisms.* San Francisco: American Association for the Advancement of Science, Pacific Division.

Butler, T. Y. 1979. *The Birds of Ecuador and the Galápagos Archipelago.* Portsmouth, N.H.: Ramphastos Agency.

Carlquist, Sherwin. 1965. *Island Life: A Natural History of the Islands of the World.* Garden City, N.Y.: Natural History Press.

*Darwin, Charles. 1859. *On the Origin of Species by Means of Natural Selection, or, The Preservation of Favored Races in the Struggle for Life.* London: John Murray.

*———. 1869. *Geological Observations on the Volcanic Islands and Parts of South America Visited during the Voyage of H. M. S. Beagle.* 3d ed. New York: D. Appleton and Co.

*———. 1871. *Journal of Researches into the Natural History and Geology of the Countries Visited during the Voyage of H. M. S. Beagle Round the World, under the Command of Captain FitzRoy, R. N.,* vol. 2. New York: Harper and Bros.

———. [1860] 1962. *The Voyage of the Beagle.* Reprint. Garden City, N.Y.: Doubleday and Co.

Eisley, Loren. 1961. *Darwin's Century: Evolution and the Men Who Discovered It.* Garden City, N.Y.: Doubleday and Co.

Farrington, B. 1982. *What Darwin Really Said.* New York: Shocken Books.

*Fisher, Albert K., and Alexander Wetmore. 1931. *Report on Birds Recorded by the Pinchot Expedition of 1929 to the Caribbean and Pacific. Proceedings of the United States National Museum,* no. 79.

Fritts, Thomas H., and Patricia R. Fritts, editors. 1982. *Race with Extinction: Herpetological Notes of J. R. Slevin's Journey to the Galápagos 1905–1906. Herpetological Monograph,* no. 1.

*Gentry, Roger L., and Gerald L. Kooyman, editors. 1986. *Fur Seals: Maternal Strategies on Land and at Sea.* Princeton, N. J.: Princeton University Press.

*Gifford, Edward Winslow. 1919. Field notes on the birds of the Galápagos Islands and of Cocos Islands, Costa Rica. *Proceedings of the California Academy of Sciences,* vol. 2:189–258.

*Gould, John. 1841. *Birds.* Part 3 of *The Zoology of the Voyage of H. M. S. Beagle, under the Command of Captain Robert FitzRoy, R. N., during the Years 1832 to 1836,* edited by Charles Darwin. London: Smith, Elder and Co.

*Grant, P. R. 1986. *Darwin's Finches.* Princeton, N.J.: Princeton University Press.

*Hamann, Ole. 1981. *Plant Communities of the Galápagos Islands. Dansk Botanisk Arkiv,* no. 34.

Harris, Michael P. 1982. *A Field Guide to the Birds of Galápagos.* 2d edition. London: William Collins Sons and Co.

Hickman, John. 1985. *The Enchanted Islands: The Galápagos Discovered.* Dover, N.H.: Tanager Books.

Himmelfarb, Gertrude. 1962. *Darwin and the Darwinian Revolution.* New York: W. W. Norton and Co.

*Lack, David. 1945. *The Galápagos finches (Geospizinae): A Study in Variation. Occasional Papers of the California Academy of Sciences,* no. 21.

*Lack, David. 1947. *Darwin's Finches: An Essay on the General Biological Theory of Evolution.* Cambridge, England: Cambridge University Press.

*Loomis, Leverett Mills. 1918. *A Review of the Albatrosses, Petrels, and Diving Petrels [of the Galápagos]. Proceedings of the California Academy of Sciences,* vol. 2:1–187.

*Martin, Paul S., and Richard G. Klein, editors. 1984. *Quaternary Extinctions: A Prehistoric Revolution.* Tucson: University of Arizona Press.

*McBirney, Alexander R., and Howel Williams. 1969. *Geology and Petrology of the Galápagos Islands. Geological Society of America Memoir,* no. 118.

Melville, Herman. 1940. *The Encantadas, or, Enchanted Isles.* With introduction, critical epilogue, and biographical notes by Victor Wolfgang von Hagen. Burlingame, Ca.: William P. Wreden.

Moore, Tui De Roy. 1982. *Galápagos: Islands Lost in Time.* With an introduction by Peter Matthiessen. New York: Viking.

Moorehead, Alan. 1969. *Darwin and the Beagle.* New York: Crescent Books.

*Moors, P. J., editor. 1985. *Conservation of Island Birds. International Council for Bird Preservation Technical Publication,* no. 3.

*Murphy, Robert Cushman. 1936. *Oceanic Birds of South America,* vols. 1 and 2. New York: American Museum of Natural History.

Nelson, Bryan. 1968. *Galápagos: Islands of Birds.* New York: William Morrow and Co.

Noticias de Galápagos. Charles Darwin Foundation for the Galápagos Islands. [45 issues published since 1963; a semi-popular account of current activities, especially concerning conservation, at the Charles Darwin Research Station and the Galápagos National Park.]

*Olson, Storrs L. 1985. The fossil record of birds. *Avian Biology,* vol. 8:79–252. New York: Academic Press.

Palmer, Ralph S. 1962. *Handbook of North American Birds.* Vol. 1, *Loons through Flamingos.* New Haven: Yale University Press.

Parker, T. A., III, S. A. Parker, and M. A. Plenge. 1982. *An Annotated Checklist of Peruvian Birds.* Vermillion, S.D.: Buteo Books.

*Perry, Roger, editor. 1984. *Galápagos.* Oxford: Pergamon Press.

Pinchot, Gifford. 1930. *To the South Seas: The Cruise of the Schooner Mary Pinchot to the Galápagos, the Marquesas, and the Tuamotu Islands and Tahiti.* Philadelphia: John C. Wilson Co.

Porter, Eliot. 1965. *Galápagos: The Flow of Wildness,* Vol. 1, *Discovery*; Vol. 2, *Prospect,* San Francisco: Sierra Club.

Pritchard, Peter C. H. 1979. *Encyclopedia of Turtles.* Jersey City, N.J.: T. F. H. Publications.

*Ridgway, Robert. 1897. Birds of the Galápagos Archipelago. *Proceedings of the United States National Museum,* no. 19:459–670.

Robinson, William A. 1936. *Voyage to the Galápagos.* New York: Harcourt, Brace and Co.

*Rothschild, Walter, and Ernest Hartert. 1899. A review of the ornithology of the Galápagos Islands, with notes on the Webster-Harris Expedition, *Novitates Zoologicae* 6:85–205.

*Simkin, Tom, Lee Siebert, Lindsay McClelland, David Bridge, Christopher Newhall, and John H. Latter. 1982. *Volcanoes of the World.* Stroudsburg, Pa.: Hutchinson Ross Publishing Co.

Simpson, George Gaylord. 1980. *Splendid Isolation: The Curious History of South American Mammals.* New Haven: Yale University Press.

Slevin, Joseph R. 1931. *Log of the Schooner "Academy" on a Voyage of Scientific Research to the Galápagos Islands, 1905–*

1906. *Occasional Papers of the California Academy of Sciences,* no. 17.

———. 1959. *The Galápagos Islands: A History of Their Exploration. Occasional Papers of the California Academy of Sciences,* no. 25.

*Snodgrass, Robert E., and Edmund Heller. 1904. *Papers from the Hopkins-Stanford Galápagos Expedition, 1898–1899.* Vol. 16, *Birds. Proceedings of the Washington Academy of Sciences,* no. 5:231–372.

*Steadman, David W. 1982. The origin of Darwin's finches. *Transactions of the San Diego Society of Natural History* 19:279–96.

*———. 1986. *Holocene Vertebrate Fossils from Isla Floreana, Galápagos. Smithsonian Contributions to Zoology,* no. 413.

*Steadman, David W., and Clayton E. Ray. 1982. *The Relationships of Megaoryzomys* curioi, *an Extinct Cricetine Rodent* (Muroidea, Muridae) *from the Galápagos Islands, Ecuador. Smithsonian Contributions to Paleobiology,* no. 51.

Sulloway, Frank J. 1982a. The *Beagle* collections of Darwin's finches (Geospizinae). *Bulletin of the British Museum (Natural History), Zoology Series* 43:49–94.

———. 1982b. Darwin and his finches: The evolution of a legend. *Journal of the History of Biology* 15:1–53.

———. 1982c. Darwin's conversion: The *Beagle* voyage and its aftermath. *Journal of the History of Biology* 15:325–96.

*Swarth, Harry S. 1931. *The Avifauna of the Galápagos Islands. Occasional Papers of the California Academy of Sciences,* no. 18.

Thornton, Ian. 1971. *Darwin's Islands: A Natural History of the Galápagos.* Garden City, N.Y.: Natural History Press.

Townsend, Charles H. 1925. The Galápagos tortoises in their relation to the whaling industry. *Zoologica* 4:55–135.

*Van Denburgh, John. 1912a. The snakes of the Galápagos Islands. *Proceedings of the California Academy of Sciences,* vol. 1:323–74.

*———. 1912b. The geckos of the Galápagos archipelago. *Proceedings of the California Academy of Sciences,* vol. 1:405–30.

*———. 1914. The gigantic land tortoises of the Galápagos Islands. *Proceedings of the California Academy of Sciences,* vol. 2:203–374.

*Van Denburgh, John, and Joseph R. Slevin. 1913. The Galápagos lizards of the genus *Tropidurus*; with notes on the iguanas of the genera *Conolophus* and *Amblyrhynchus. Proceedings of the California Academy of Sciences,* vol. 2:133–202.

Wafer, Lionel. [1699] 1903. *A New Voyage and Description of the Isthmus of America.* Edited by George Parker Winship. Cleveland: Burrows Brothers.

Watson, George. 1975. *Birds of the Antarctic and Sub-Antarctic. Antarctic Research Series,* vol. 24. Washington, D.C.: American Geophysical Union.

White, Alan. 1972. *Galápagos Guide.* Quito, Ecuador: Imprenta Europa.

Picture Credits

SIL indicates Smithsonian Institution Libraries.

Endpapers
Adapted from an original map by Denys Baker published in John Treherne, *The Galapagos Affair,* copyright © 1983 by Dr. J. E. Treherne. Reprinted by permission of Jonathan Cape, London, and Random House, New York.

Front Matter
Page 1 Tui De Roy; 2–3 Nathan Farb, image reversed with permission (*The Galápagos,* a collection of Nathan Farb's photographic work in the islands, will be published by Rizzoli, New York, in 1989); 4–5 D. and M. Littler; 6 Tui De Roy; 8 D. and M. Littler; 10 D. and M. Littler; 11 upper and lower right, D. and M. Littler; 12–13 Nathan Farb, see 2–3 above; 14 Kjell B. Sandved, Smithsonian Institution; 16 art by Lee M. Steadman; 18 Lee M. Steadman; 21 David L. Clark.

Part One
Page 23 art by John Gould from *The Zoology of the Voyage of H.M.S. Beagle,* vol. 2, part 3, plate 41, 1980 facsimile edition, SIL.

Chapter One
Page 25 David O. Johnson; 27 D. and M. Littler; 28 Ambrose Cowley, *Collection of Original Voyages,* reprinted from *Galapagos,* ed. R. Perry, 1984, courtesy of Pergamon Press; 29 Kjell B. Sandved, Smithsonian Institution; 30–31 D. and M. Littler; 31 right, from A. E. Brehm, *Merveilles de la nature—Les reptiles et les batraciens,* 1885, SIL; 32 Barbara S. Tuceling.

Chapter Two
Page 35 D. and M. Littler; 37 top, Tui De Roy; 37 map by Ellen Paige, courtesy of David Steadman; 38 diagram by Roberta Voteary; 39 top, Barbara S. Tuceling; 39 bottom, art by Lee M. Steadman; 40 D. and M. Littler; 41 top, from *Curtis's Botanical Magazine,* vol. 108, plate 6637, 1882, SIL; 41 bottom, D. and M. Littler; 43 David O. Johnson.

Chapter Three
Page 45 D. and M. Littler; 46 courtesy of Down House, The Royal College of Surgeons; 47 David O. Johnson; 48–49 *The Beagle in Murray Narrow,* watercolor by Conrad Martens, courtesy of Down House, The Royal College of Surgeons; 50 from *The Zoology of the Voyage of H.M.S. Beagle,* vol. 1, part 1, plate 1, 1980 facsimile edition, SIL; 51 David L. Clark; 52 from *Narra-*

tive of the Surveying Voyages of His Majesty's Ships Adventure and Beagle between the Years 1826 and 1836, vol. 2, 1839, SIL; 53 from Charles Darwin, *Journal of Researches into the Natural History and Geology of the Countries Visited during the Voyage of H.M.S. Beagle around the World,* 1845, SIL; 54 David O. Johnson; 55 art by John Gould from *The Zoology of the Voyage of H.M.S. Beagle,* vol. 2, part 3, plate 46, 1980 facsimile edition, SIL; 56 courtesy of Down House, The Royal College of Surgeons; 57 courtesy of Down House, The Royal College of Surgeons; 59 ©BM (NH), photograph by John Downs, courtesy of British Museum (Natural History).

Chapter Four
Page 61 Tui De Roy; 62 from Walter Rothschild, *Extinct Birds,* plate 26, 1907, SIL; 63 D. and M. Littler; 64 art by Lee M. Steadman; 65 top and bottom, James R. Hill, III; 67 top and bottom, James R. Hill, III; 68 David Steadman; 71 from David Lack, *Darwin's Finches,* copyright © 1983, Cambridge University Press, reprinted with permission; 72 from Walter Rothschild, *Extinct Birds,* plate 4, 1907, SIL; 74 art by Guy Tudor; 75 Melissa Graybeal.

Chapter Five
Page 77 David O. Johnson; 78 Melissa Graybeal; 79 Robert P. Reynolds; 80 Robert P. Reynolds; 81 Barbara S. Tuceling; 83 D. and M. Littler; 84 Gary R. Robinson; 86 top, Melissa Graybeal; 86 bottom, Robert P. Reynolds; 87 Robert P. Reynolds; 89 D. and M. Littler; 90 David L. Clark.

Part Two
Page 91 art by John Gould from *The Zoology of the Voyage of H.M.S. Beagle,* vol. 2, part 3, plate 37, 1980 facsimile edition, SIL.

Introduction to the Plates
Page 93 David O. Johnson; 94 Lori Steadman; 95 D. and M. Littler; 96–97 David O. Johnson; 97 bottom, art by Lee M. Steadman; 99 art by John Gould from *The Zoology of the Voyage of H.M.S. Beagle,* vol. 2, part 3, plate 43, 1980 facsimile edition, SIL.

Back Matter
Page 208 D. and M. Littler.